Implementing Proactive Environmental Management

Lessons Learned from Best Commercial Practice

Frank Camm

Jeffrey A. Drezner

Beth E. Lachman

Susan A. Resetar

T0159559

Prepared for the
Office of the Secretary of Defense

National Defense Research Institute

RAND

The research described in this report was conducted for the Office of the Deputy Under Secretary of Defense for Environmental Security within the Acquisition and Technology Policy Center of RAND's National Defense Research Institute, a federally funded research and development center sponsored by the Office of the Secretary of Defense, the Joint Staff, the Unified Commands, and the defense agencies under Contract DASW01-01-C-0004.

Library of Congress Cataloging-in-Publication Data

Implementing proactive environmental management : lessons learned from best
    commercial practice / Frank Camm ... [et al.].
       p. cm.
    "MR-1371."
    Includes bibliographical references.
    ISBN 0-8330-3015-9
    1. United States. Dept. of Defense—Procurement—Environmental aspects. 2.
Defense contracts—Environmental aspects—United States. 3. Environmental
management—United States. 4. United States. Dept. of Defense. I. Camm,
Frank A., 1949–

UC263 .I44 2001
363.7'05—dc21

2001031897

RAND is a nonprofit institution that helps improve policy and decisionmaking through research and analysis. RAND® is a registered trademark. RAND's publications do not necessarily reflect the opinions or policies of its research sponsors.

Published 2001 by RAND
1700 Main Street, P.O. Box 2138, Santa Monica, CA 90407-2138
1200 South Hayes Street, Arlington, VA 22202-5050
201 North Craig Street, Suite 102, Pittsburgh, PA 15213
RAND URL: http://www.rand.org/
To order RAND documents or to obtain additional information,
contact Distribution Services: Telephone: (310) 451-7002;
Fax: (310) 451-6915; Email: order@rand.org

Since 1985, a new approach to environmental management has emerged among innovative organizations and regulators. It draws on broader efforts to induce organizational learning to improve production and management processes on a continuing basis. The new approach views environmental management not simply in terms of requirements to comply with specific rules and regulations in place today but rather in terms of ways to adjust product designs, production and delivery processes, and organizational behaviors over time to cut the total social costs associated with environmental emissions and, where possible, turn environmental issues to strategic advantage for the organizations involved.

The Department of Defense (DoD) has participated in this new approach and wants to continue its role as a proactive innovator, seeking to improve the nation's environment in ways that are compatible with its primary responsibility to provide for the national defense. To maintain its awareness of analogous efforts among commercial firms, the Office of the Deputy Under Secretary of Defense for Environmental Security asked RAND to review new environmental management programs in the commercial sector relevant to weapon system design, provision of central logistics services, integration of different defense activities on installations, and management of cleanup programs.

Early work on the project revealed that DoD's general policies on environmental management were compatible with policies being developed by leading firms with activities analogous to those in these four areas. In response, the deputy under secretary asked RAND to focus on effective *implementation* of such environmental management policies. To do this, we initiated case studies of environmental management in two leading firms relevant to each of the four policy areas above. These case studies have allowed us to examine environmental policies and to understand how specific organizations have integrated these policies with their broader corporate cultures. We have found that such integration lies at the heart of successful implementation of environmental management policies.

We have documented our work to date in the following: Resetar, Camm, and Drezner (1998); Drezner and Camm (1999); Camm (2001); Lachman, Camm, and Resetar (2001). This report summarizes our findings from the secondary literature and the case studies documented in the reports above.

This research was conducted for the Office of the Deputy Under Secretary of Defense for Environmental Security within the Acquisition and Technology Policy Center of RAND's National Defense Research Institute, a federally funded research and development center sponsored by the Office of the Secretary of Defense, the Joint Staff, the Unified Commands, and the defense agencies.

CONTENTS

Preface iii

Tables.. vii

Examples ix

Summary xi

Acknowledgments................................ xix

Abbreviations xxi

Chapter One
    INTRODUCTION 1

Chapter Two
    ANALYTIC APPROACH 5

Chapter Three
    CENTRAL POLICY CHALLENGE: INTEGRATE
    ENVIRONMENTAL MISSIONS AND FUNCTIONS WITH
    CORE MISSIONS AND FUNCTIONS 9
    Identify Stakeholders and Related Goals 12
    Maintain Senior Leadership Support 13
    Give Environmental Champions Day-to-Day
        Responsibility 14
    Build Coalitions with Other Internal Interests 16
    Integrate Relevant Elements of the Value Chain 17
    State Environmental Goals in Simple, Specific Terms 19
    Use Cross-Functional Teams for Specific Decisions,
        Projects, and Processes 20

Develop Tools to Identify Firmwide Effects of
Environmentally Related Activities   22
Balance Centralization and Decentralization   23
Implications for DoD   25

Chapter Four
CENTRAL IMPLEMENTATION CHALLENGE 1: THERE
ARE NO SILVER BULLETS WHEN EVERY SITUATION
IS DIFFERENT   27
Motivate Creative and Persistent Change Agents   28
Assign Responsibilities Clearly Throughout the Firm   29
Design Metrics to Motivate the Right Behavior   30
Use Incentives to Motivate the Right Behavior   33
Manage Failures to Limit Disincentives for Risk-Taking . .   35
Empower Employees with Formal Training   35
Develop a Supportive Organizational Context for Tools . .   37
Communicate Continuously in All Directions   39
Manage Relationships with Stakeholders   40
Benchmark to Promote Continuous Improvement   43

Chapter Five
CENTRAL IMPLEMENTATION CHALLENGE 2: RADICAL
ORGANIZATIONAL CHANGE TAKES A LONG TIME   45

Chapter Six
RECOMMENDATION: USE FORMAL QUALITY
FRAMEWORKS TO IMPLEMENT AN INTEGRATION
POLICY   49
Available Formal Quality Frameworks   50
Formal Quality Frameworks for DoD   59

Bibliography   63

TABLES

1. Use Formal Quality Frameworks to Support the
   Key Policy Challenge: Integrate Environmental
   Missions and Functions with Core Missions and
   Functions   54
2. Use Formal Quality Frameworks to Support
   Implementation Challenge 1: There Are No
   Silver Bullets When Every Situation Is Different   56
3. Use Formal Quality Frameworks to Support
   Implementation Challenge 2: Radical
   Organizational Change Takes a Long Time   58

1. Procter & Gamble: Justifying Environmental
   Actions   10
2. WDWR: Governing the Wetlands via the 20-Year
   Permit   11
3. Volvo: Strategic Goal-Setting and Target-Setting   12
4. Procter & Gamble: Community Interview
   Program   13
5. Volvo: Environmental Competency Center   14
6. Hewlett-Packard: Strategic Metrics for
   Decisionmaking   14
7. Hewlett-Packard: Environmental Stewardship
   Program   15
8. WDWR: Cost Savings Through "Environmentality" . .   16
9. DuPont and Olin: Views on Internal and External
   Sources   17
10. IBM and Ford: Views on Using ISO 14001 to
    Qualify Suppliers   18
11. Procter & Gamble: Influencing Suppliers'
    Environmental Performance   18
12. Ford: Environmental Performance Targets in the
    Business Plan   19
13. Procter & Gamble: Allocating Environmental
    Costs   20
14. DuPont: Corporate Remediation Group   21
15. Olin: Team-Based Decisionmaking   21
16. Volvo: Environmental Priorities Strategies
    System   22
17. Hewlett-Packard: Environmental Database   23

18. DuPont and Olin: Centralized Remediation
    Programs 24
19. Volvo: Views on Affecting Automobile
    Environmental Performance 27
20. DuPont: Aligning Environmental Concerns
    with Business Priorities 28
21. WDWR: Environmental Responsibility at the
    Contemporary Hotel 30
22. Olin: Metrics for Managing Remediation 31
23. Hewlett-Packard: Guidelines for Developing
    Metrics 31
24. Procter & Gamble: Key Element Assessment
    Audits 32
25. WDWR: Nonmonetary Incentives at WDWR 34
26. Volvo: Environmental Training Program 36
27. DuPont: Remediation Information System 37
28. Hewlett-Packard: Developing Life-Cycle
    Assessment Tools 38
29. Volvo: Developing the Environmental Priorities
    Strategies System 39
30. Olin: Relationships with External Stakeholders 41
31. Procter & Gamble: Relationships with External
    Stakeholders 42
32. WDWR: Working with External Stakeholders
    on the 20-Year Permit 42
33. Ford: A Staged Approach for Global
    Registration to ISO 14001 47
34. Ford and IBM: Choosing Third-Party
    Registration to ISO 14001 52
35. IBM: Single Worldwide Registration to ISO 14001 ... 60

From 1990 to 1995, as the total defense budget fell from $315 to 291 billion a year, DoD environmental spending rose to $5.2 billion a year. At the same time, increasingly tight environmental regulations constrained training and vessel mobility in DoD, potentially limiting military readiness. These trends brought environmental management into high focus. Was DoD making appropriate trade-offs among (1) its military mission, (2) its environmental obligations, and (3) constraints on its budget and other resources? Were there opportunities to increase military performance without compromising environmental obligations or resource constraints?

During the 1980s and early 1990s, many U.S. firms found themselves in a similar situation. Even as their environmental obligations were rising in the face of increasingly demanding regulations and threats of liability, increasingly effective global competition squeezed their profit margins, forcing these firms to think about environmental management in a different way.

The Office of the Deputy Under Secretary of Defense for Environmental Security asked RAND to study the environmental management practices of commercial firms recognized as having the best practices of this kind. Such practices should provide lessons that DoD could use to improve its own environmental management practices. This report summarizes the findings of the study that resulted from this request.

ANALYTIC APPROACH

The analysis underlying this report focused on environmental management issues relevant to four key policy areas in DoD: the design, development, and modification of weapon systems; the management of central logistics activities; the integration of environmental issues associated with different activities on installations; and the management of cleanup programs. Preliminary analysis revealed that DoD's existing environmental management policies were compatible with the policies of commercial firms recognized by their peers to have the most innovative environmental management policies. But these firms were learning valuable lessons about *implementing* these policies—translating them into concrete programs and beneficial outcomes—that could benefit the department. To understand how leading firms were implementing their new policies, we identified two firms involved in activities analogous to those in each of the four key policy areas in DoD. We conducted case studies for each of these firms. The case studies provided information on the organizational contexts of the implementations, information critical to any effort to transfer these lessons from a commercial setting to the setting in which DoD operates.

CENTRAL POLICY CHALLENGE: INTEGRATE ENVIRONMENTAL MISSIONS AND FUNCTIONS WITH CORE MISSIONS AND FUNCTIONS

The central lesson of these case studies and the broader secondary literature on environmental management is that successful implementation depends on an organization's ability to integrate its environmental management program with the management system it uses to plan and execute its core missions and functions. Success occurs when managers come to view environmental issues as simply one more context in which they can pursue the core values of the organization.

Successful integration depends on the organization's ability to treat environmental concerns the same way it treats questions it considers to be closer to its core concerns. Hence, it must be able to

- identify how environmental issues affect its key stakeholders and how these issues relate to stakeholder goals

- develop and sustain senior leadership support for proactive treatment of environmental issues
- identify champions who can take day-to-day responsibility for managing environmental issues to satisfy the specific stakeholder goals that the senior leadership has endorsed
- make environmental principals in the organization effective partners in coalitions in the organization to align environmental interests with other specialized interests
- after identifying the organization's position in the value chains that it services, work with other elements of these value chains to achieve common goals
- state specific environmental goals in simple terms that help individual decisionmakers relate them to broader corporate goals without much ambiguity
- for specific decisions or projects, use teams that include representatives of all the relevant functions, including environmental representatives when appropriate
- promote routine use of databases and analytic tools that help decisionmakers see how environmental decisions affect all parts of the organization
- balance centralization and decentralization to align environmental concerns with the most closely related core activities.

Taken together, such initiatives attempt to link environmental concerns to every part of the organization where decisions can affect them without diluting environmental policy so much that it becomes everyone's responsibility and therefore no one's responsibility. An effective organization must retain its environmental focus in the form of champions and principals who can be held accountable. But these specialists must view their environmental mission through the clear lens of the broader corporate goals and culture, as embodied in the organization's stakeholders and senior leadership. And these specialists must appreciate that they cannot be effective if they isolate themselves within the organization. They must reach out to colleagues with other particular interests in the organization and communicate with them using data and language that their colleagues understand and respect because the data and language are compatible with the organization's core values and processes.

CENTRAL IMPLEMENTATION CHALLENGE 1: THERE ARE NO SILVER BULLETS WHEN EVERY SITUATION IS DIFFERENT

When environmental concerns pervade an organization, they must be handled the way every other management problem is: one situation at a time. The organization faces precisely the same problem here that it faces when it asks what it can do to improve its general performance. And the same ideas that help organizations improve general performance can help them implement a more proactive approach to environmental management. To be successful, an organization seeks to

- motivate employees to be not only creative but also dogged in their determination to change the status quo for the better

- assign responsibilities clearly so that specific individuals or teams feel the effects of environmental decisions on the organization as a whole and can be held accountable for promoting the goals of the organization as a whole over the long term

- design metrics to encourage individuals and teams, constrained as they are in their particular locations in the organization, to make decisions compatible with the organization's broad goals

- back up these metrics with incentives that are compatible with the organization's broader norms about compensation and advancement

- expect individual failures to occur when employees push hard enough for real change and (1) limit the damage from such failures while (2) helping employees learn from these failures rather than punishing them for failing[1]

- train employees to increase their environmental awareness and improve their ability to work collaboratively. Design training so that it occurs "just in time," when employees need it to execute specific tasks

- provide effective analytic tools and maintain a supportive organizational environment for their use

_____

[1]This is perhaps the most challenging goal listed here.

- communicate continuously, internally and with key stakeholders, to sustain trust and commitment
- benchmark environmental performance against that of other organizations, report the results to the senior leadership, and use the results to sustain senior-level support for continuing improvement in environmental performance.

Each of these activities touches the people who have traditionally been associated with environmental management in an organization. But these activities are most effective when they occur throughout the organization, benefiting environmental management and hence performance in the process. A strong trend among successful commercial firms indicates that, while they adopt practices and policies like these to promote general improvement, they discover only after the fact that policies designed, say, to boost profits can also easily improve environmental performance. Improved environmental performance is almost a side effect until these organizations see the connection and focus activities of this kind on specific environmental goals. But even when an environmental focus develops, effective integration demands that such organizations approach environmental concerns from a broader organizational perspective.

CENTRAL IMPLEMENTATION CHALLENGE 2: RADICAL ORGANIZATIONAL CHANGE TAKES A LONG TIME

The organizational policies discussed above typically require dramatic change in the way an organization does business. Major change takes time and commitment and becomes more difficult as organizations grow. DoD's size and the relative instability in its leadership over time present special challenges beyond those that most successful commercial organizations have faced. But DoD also has a tradition of managing and achieving dramatic change in the weapon systems it designs and deploys. The same management methods used to oversee the innovation associated with major weapon system developments offer cues and paradigms that DoD could exploit to pursue the kind of organizational innovation discussed here.

In particular, successful organizations benefit from recognizing that change will take time. They develop formal programs with explicit milestones and goals that can be adjusted as change proceeds and as knowledge accumulates. They sequence change carefully within such programs. They start with problems that are not critical to their core concerns and hence do not present serious risks if failures occur. Nonetheless, these organizations recognize that, despite their best efforts and intentions, individual failures early in a program of change can threaten the whole program. They start with simple problems and move toward more-complex ones as they accumulate knowledge and experience. Within these constraints, they seek pilot changes that they can learn from. With this in mind, they "seed" innovations across organizations and/or functions so that each individual change provides an effective basis for additional changes in related activities.

In the end, large-scale organizational change presents immense challenges and uncertainties. An organization can rarely see its end state clearly when it starts such a change process. But successful organizations have demonstrated that careful management of change, to limit the cost of failures and learn from those that occur, is possible. Such management uses basic principles that the DoD acquisition community understands well.

RECOMMENDATION: USE FORMAL QUALITY FRAMEWORKS TO IMPLEMENT AN INTEGRATION POLICY

The long time lines, the pervasive but diffuse effects throughout a very large organization, and the need to affect how individuals conduct their daily routine of management and decisionmaking within a large, diverse organization challenge the reformer's natural desire for focus and clear direction. Seen in this light, proactive environmental management looks as elusive as total quality management did to U.S. firms trying and repeatedly failing to emulate innovative Japanese business practices before 1980. Repeated attempts and failures left most U.S. firms and their employees jaded and wary of prescriptions that were too ephemeral to grasp. The parallel between proactive environmental management and total quality management is relevant for two reasons.

First, broadly writ, the policies and practices discussed above are in fact closely associated with total quality management. Taken together, they come very close to defining what management consultants mean when they prescribe the use of total quality management.

So the parallel is more than coincidental. Increasingly, proactive commercial firms describe their environmental management policies as simple applications or extensions of their quality programs to the specific concerns of the environmental manager. In fact, the most successful firms adopt total quality management as a basic corporate tenet. To integrate environmental management with their core management concerns, they must then apply quality methods to their environmental issues.

Second, organizations struggling with the ephemeral nature of total quality management have found success in formalized frameworks that help them understand how well they are doing when they try quality methods and what they need to do to get better. Analogous frameworks have been developed to help organizations cope with the demands of implementing proactive environmental management practices like those discussed above. That is, the broad descriptions of proactive policies and practices become concrete and tangible in the context of these new frameworks.

International Standards Organization (ISO) 9000 offers the simplest quality-based framework. It is a management standard that firms pursue by asking a third party to audit their operations and certify that they are using what are in effect quality-based procedures. ISO 9000 has been so successful in instilling quality methods that firms must achieve such certification to be qualified as suppliers in many industries; demand for such certification continues to grow rapidly.

ISO 14000 has recently emerged as a parallel management standard that focuses on environmental management procedures. It is not nearly as demanding as ISO 9000 but does provide a similarly well-defined template that defines whether or not an organization has implemented proactive environmental management. The designers of ISO 9000 and 14000 expect the two to be effectively integrated over time as experience grows with both. Today, ISO 9000 certification is typically a necessary stepping stone toward ISO 14000 certification.

The Malcolm Baldrige Award presents a more-challenging quality standard. Where ISO 9000 has become an entry-level standard defining minimal expectations about the use of quality methods, the Baldrige Award forces organizations to compete against one another and against extremely demanding objective criteria that define clearly where an organization stands and what it needs to do next to improve its use of a quality-based approach to management. Firms that seek the Baldrige Award testify that the effort teaches them a great deal. Since the Baldrige was first awarded in 1988, the share values of its winners have outperformed those of organizations that applied but did not win; the share values of firms that have at least applied for the award have outperformed the stock market at large. The Council of Great Lakes Industries has developed a variant of the Baldrige Award criteria that organizations can use to assess their implementation of proactive environmental management.

Such formal frameworks offer DoD tangible ways to assess its efforts to introduce total quality management more broadly and proactive environmental management in particular. Continuing demands to improve the processes in the defense infrastructure will sustain support for introducing quality methods much more broadly in DoD than they have been to date. Introducing proactive environmental management could be a natural adjunct to a broader DoD program of process improvement. As a policy area distant from DoD's core missions and functions, environmental management might even serve as an appropriate place to pilot quality-based management methods. DoD's environmental community could serve its own interests while simultaneously marching in the vanguard of the growing effort to improve processes departmentwide. Such a role would be a logical extension of the commitment the DoD environmental community has already made to proactive environmental management policy principles.

ACKNOWLEDGMENTS

Gary D. Vest, Principal Assistant Deputy Under Secretary of Defense (Environmental Security), suggested and supported RAND's study of proactive environmental management practices in commercial firms. Patrick Meehan, Jr., Director of Program Integration for the Deputy Under Secretary of Defense (Environmental Security), was the program officer for this study. Both provided useful suggestions and feedback, as well as ready access to relevant staffs in the Office of the Secretary of Defense and the Military Departments. Discussions with knowledgeable people in environmental activities throughout DoD helped us focus our exploration of commercial practices on the issues of greatest importance to DoD.

Within RAND, D. J. Peterson's reviews of most of the products of this work, including this final one, have significantly improved their quality. Quality, implementation, and defense resource specialists at RAND helped us think about proactive environmental management in the broader context of implementing new defense resource policies in a post–Cold War defense environment. We thank especially Beth Benjamin, Susan Bodilly, John Bondanella, Mary Chenoweth, I. K. Cohen, Shan Cretin, James Dertouzos, William Hix, Sarah Hunter, Brent Keltner, Jeff Luck, Gary Massey, Louis Miller, Nancy Moore, Daniel Norton, Raymond Pyles, David Rubenson, H. L. Shulman, Giles Smith, and Anny Wong. Phyllis Gilmore edited the document.

We thank them all, but retain full responsibility for the accuracy and analytic soundness of the material presented here.

ABBREVIATIONS

BRAC	Base Realignment and Closure
DoD	Department of Defense
DSB	Defense Science Board
EPA	Environmental Protection Agency
EMAS	European Eco-Management and Audit Scheme
GEMI	Global Environmental Management Initiative
HP	Hewlett-Packard
ISO	International Standards Organization
OSD	Office of the Secretary of Defense
P&G	Procter & Gamble
PRP	Primary responsible party
R&D	Research and development
SPO	System acquisition program office
TQEM	Total quality environmental management
TQM	Total quality management
WDWR	Walt Disney World Resort

Chapter One

INTRODUCTION

From 1990 to 1995, as the total defense budget fell from $315 to 291 billion a year, the Department of Defense's (DoD's) environmental spending rose to $5.2 billion a year.[1] At the same time, increasingly tight environmental regulations constrained training and vessel mobility in DoD, potentially limiting military readiness. These trends brought environmental management into high focus. Was DoD making appropriate trade-offs among (1) its military mission, (2) its environmental obligations, and (3) constraints on its budget and other resources? Were there opportunities to increase military performance without compromising environmental obligations or resource constraints? Election of a Republican-majority House of Representatives in 1994 only heightened these concerns as Congress scrutinized the defense budget for opportunities to eliminate any spending that did not contribute directly to the department's national security mission.

During the 1980s and early 1990s, many U.S. firms found themselves in a similar situation. Even as their environmental obligations were rising in the face of increasingly demanding regulations and threats of liability, increasingly effective global competition squeezed their profit margins, forcing these firms to think about environmental management in a different way. A 1995 DSB study recognized this parallel:

---

[1]Environmental expenditures are from Defense Science Board (DSB) (1995), p. 9; DoD expenditures are from U.S. Bureau of the Census (1996), Table 517.

1

Almost all premier private sector firms are providing environmental leadership. They are finding opportunities for cost savings through prudent environmental management, technology investments, and pollution prevention. They are also involving local and state stakeholders in their decisions. This proactive management approach is not pursued for altruistic reasons. The management[s] of these companies are convinced that they can reduce environmental costs in the long run, have greater flexibility in their operations and, hence, gain competitive advantages through such an approach.

The Task Force believes that the Department faces a similar set of decisions. If the DoD takes a proactive leadership position—working with stakeholders, pursuing new technology and pollution prevention, leveraging its buying power, and pursuing the significant risks first—it will be in a much stronger position to assure US national security interests. . . . It will be cheaper in the long run to meet its requirements in a proactive fashion than to be forced to do so through protracted regulatory proceedings at the state and local levels. (DSB, 1995, p. ES-1.)

The Office of the Deputy Under Secretary of Defense for Environmental Security asked RAND to study the environmental management practices of commercial firms recognized as having the best practices of this kind in the country. Such practices should provide lessons that DoD could use to improve its own environmental management practices. This report summarizes the findings of the study that resulted from this request.[2]

The report first summarizes RAND's analytic approach in Chapter Two. Chapter Three identifies the central policy challenge of proactive environmental management—integrating environmental missions and functions with core missions and functions.[3] The Office of the Secretary of Defense (OSD) is already familiar with the key high-level policy issues that proactive commercial firms associate with

---

[2]For more-detailed findings and documentation, see Resetar, Camm, and Drezner (1998); Drezner and Camm (1999); Camm, (2001); and Lachman, Camm, and Resetar (2001).

[3]By *core*, we mean the activities that are central to the firm's *raison d'être* and continuing success as a viable firm. These are the activities that the senior leadership and management of the firm spend the majority of their time on. Such core activities may or may not correspond to *core* as it is often discussed in a DoD setting.

such an integration effort. Implementing this kind of policy remains a serious challenge for OSD. In fact, implementation raises two major challenges. First, no silver bullet is available for implementing proactive environmental management throughout DoD. The problem of implementation must be addressed in the context of each particular setting in the department. Chapter Four discusses this point. Second, radical organizational change takes a long time. DoD will need to institutionalize a process of change that will extend beyond the term of any one leadership team. Chapter Five discusses this point. Proactive commercial firms have struggled with both of these challenges. Chapter Six summarizes the lessons learned from commercial experience and recommends that DoD consider adopting an approach that many proactive commercial firms have found to be useful: using total quality management to implement environmental management policy and, more specifically, applying one or more formal quality-based frameworks, described below.

Interspersed throughout the text are examples drawn from the eight primary case studies underlying this analysis. These examples illustrate the principles discussed in the text around them. At least as important, they help demonstrate how these principles operate together in specific organizational contexts. The proactive environmental management practices discussed in these examples almost always operate synergistically with one another. As a result, the examples often relate to ideas presented throughout the report and could have been placed in any of several places. Put another way, the practical issues addressed in these examples often provide counterpoint to the more-general ideas in the text immediately around them. This counterpoint should emphasize that it is hard in practice to isolate the implementation of individual elements of proactive practice, or their effects, from one another.

The examples offered were current when we observed them over the last few years. We have found that practices often evolve fairly quickly in the commercial world. So, although the specific practices described may still be in place, we always describe them here in the past tense.

Chapter Two

ANALYTIC APPROACH

RAND first reviewed DoD's environmental management program by reading high-level DoD documents, interviewing environmental officials in the armed services, and visiting several representative bases. This review revealed two things.

First, DoD's high-level environmental management *policy* already reflected many of the practices that were proving successful in commercial firms. DoD's primary challenge was less one of knowing what to do than of understanding how to *implement* this policy in a very large organization. Hence, the information DoD needed most from the commercial sector was how proactive firms had implemented the key elements of their environmental management programs.

Second, among the many environmental activities that DoD pursues, four are particularly important:

- managing the design and development of new weapon systems and subsystems—and modifications to them—so that they will have cost-effective environmental performance levels over their lifetimes

- managing the industrial processes in central logistics activities so that they balance military, environmental, and cost constraints appropriately in the support of existing weapon systems

- managing the many, diverse, environmentally relevant activities on installations in an integrated way to comply with current regulations and prevent future pollution cost-effectively

- managing the programs responsible for remediating waste-disposal sites on active bases, bases being closed through Base Realignment and Closure (BRAC) reviews, and other sites where DoD is a primary responsible party (PRP).

RAND focused on these four areas. For each area, we conducted an in-depth review of the recent academic, policy, and trade literatures. We used these literatures to construct general descriptions of best practices in the commercial sector and to identify individual firms for more in-depth analysis. Proactive environmental management is not as prevalent among commercial firms as the DSB study suggests.[1] But the most proactive firms are developing and implementing very innovative practices. Like DoD, they are finding that implementation is more challenging than policy development.

In each area, we chose two firms where we could study in depth the implementation of best practices in the context of specific organizations. Because the success of implementation depends heavily on the fine details of how a policy or practice fits in a particular organizational culture, the organizational setting is important to understand. This is important for understanding why a particular practice worked in the original setting and for understanding what DoD must consider when transferring this practice to its own setting. These literature reviews and case studies then provided the basis for developing lessons learned for DoD.

We focused on the following firms:

- design and acquisition of new systems: Hewlett-Packard (HP), Volvo

- central logistics: Ford, IBM

- integrated facility management: Procter & Gamble (P&G) Paper Products Company, Walt Disney World Resort (WDWR)

- management of waste-site remediation: DuPont, Olin.

In each literature review and case study, we have paid special attention to activities normally associated with proactive environmental

---

[1]See, for example, the survey results reported in "The Green Machine" (1995), Greeno et al. (1996), and Nagel (1994).

management, in DoD and elsewhere. In particular, we have focused on

- designing general environmental management systems, including metrics, to ensure integration
- training and motivating people
- providing tools and information to support the environmental mission
- promoting effective relationships with relevant stakeholders
- the implications of future International Standards Organization (ISO) 14000 implementation.[2]

We have verified the importance of these basic elements of environmental management to the most proactive firms and have developed more-detailed information on how proactive firms are implementing policies relevant to each of these elements.

---

[2]ISO 14000 is a series of proposed international guidelines that could become standards for formal environmental management systems in individual organizations and could shape DoD's regulatory environment in the future. The first guideline in this series, ISO 14001, was issued in 1996.

Chapter Three

CENTRAL POLICY CHALLENGE: INTEGRATE ENVIRONMENTAL MISSIONS AND FUNCTIONS WITH CORE MISSIONS AND FUNCTIONS

Rubenson et al. (1994) highlighted the degree of separation between combat and environmental cultures in the U.S. Army and the importance of finding ways to eliminate this separation. This problem has been as important in commercial firms as it is in DoD today. Large firms face complex environmental regulations that they must obey, to the satisfaction of their regulators, before they have an effective license to pursue the core interests of their trade. Large firms have developed large, specialized staffs to manage this environmental problem. These specialists have sought to keep regulators satisfied while the rest of the employees of the firm sought profits. Environmental and other employees faced very different decision environments and hence had a limited need to interact. Traditional regulation has reinforced this difference by specifying much of what firms must do to comply with the law in close detail.

Leading commercial firms began to think about their environmental concerns differently in the 1980s.[1] Three factors are mentioned repeatedly:

1. As regulations became more complex, large firms turned to increasingly complex internal audits to verify that they were in compliance with the law. As potential liability for environmental

---

[1]For a good overview, see Ehrfeld and Howard (1995) or Piasecki (1995). For a useful exchange of views among leading corporate executives and environmental specialists, see Porter and van den Linde (1995), Walley and Whitehead (1994), and Clarke et al. (1994). For a recent academic overview of these issues, see Starik, Marcus, and Ilinitsch (2000).

damages grew, these firms wanted more information on their exposure. To collect this information, environmental specialists had to become increasingly knowledgeable about the core activities of their firms and the information systems these firms used to manage their core activities. These audits brought home how pervasive the effects of regulation were and how important it was to recognize environmental management in the context of everything a firm did.

2. Large firms came increasingly to recognize that they could not reverse environmental regulation and that, as the effects of regulation affected their activities more pervasively, a more-constructive approach to dealing with their environmental problems would be more cost-effective. Such major events as the catastrophic release of toxic chemicals in Bhopal, India, in 1984 drove home the fact that simply complying is not always enough to avoid serious corporate liability. A belief that the burden of environmental regulation was only likely to increase in unpredictable ways led an increasing number of firms to ask whether there was some way to avoid regulation in the first place by getting rid of the chemicals that forced them into contact with regulators.

Example 1

Procter & Gamble: Justifying Environmental Actions

P&G sought, where possible, to link environmental decisions to quantitative cost-benefit assessments but recognized that less-quantitative, strategic arguments were also relevant, particularly when they did not require significant investments. Similarly, in a corporate culture that sought to reduce complexity, P&G recognized that any chemical emission tends to increase process complexity by inviting potential regulatory intrusion. P&G argued that proactive environmental policy protected P&G's long-term franchise to conduct business as strategically as possible. This gave P&G the flexibility to develop its own solutions to environmental problems. It helped build trust with regulators and the local community, supporting mutually attractive partnerships that reduced P&G's compliance costs and reduced external constraints over the long run. This perspective led P&G to reduce its use of chlorine and ammonium nitrogen and to address odor problems raised by the community, even though regulators required no actions on these issues.

3. A few pioneers began to demonstrate that a constructive approach to environmental management could in fact reduce the effects of regulation on companies. A proactive approach allowed firms to save money by reducing the resources used and the pollution generated and to negotiate effectively with regulators to find mutually attractive solutions to environmental problems.

Integration of environmental and core concerns lies very close to the heart of this new corporate view. Better information about the environmental aspects of their day-to-day activities and a growing recognition that they could deal effectively with many environmental concerns by changing their day-to-day activities led a growing number of large firms to seek better ways to do this. By 1990, many experiments were under way in different firms, and more have begun every year since. Federal and state regulators have promoted this new approach by encouraging large firms to take voluntary actions to reduce emissions and to become more proactive in suggesting cost-effective ways to improve environmental performance.

Example 2

WDWR: Governing the Wetlands via the 20-Year Permit

WDWR reached agreements with the Florida Department of Environmental Protection, U.S. Army Corps of Engineers, U.S. Fish and Wildlife Service, and several other agencies for a 20-year permit governing wetlands on the entire 31,000-acre WDWR property. As part of the agreement, Disney agreed to affect only 446 acres of wetlands in its development of the property; purchase nearby ecologically sensitive land; donate 8,500 acres to the Nature Conservancy, with the funds to manage it for 20 years, as a large-scale wetlands mitigation and preserve area; and place permanent conservation easements on 7,500 acres of its property, guaranteeing that the land would remain in its natural state. Disney invested $40 million in creating these agreements based on an internal assessment that they would pay for themselves by allowing Disney to avoid piecemeal permitting processes and would increase the value of development permitted on the property. Disney's senior leadership tracked the effort closely through its lifetime. The agreements have paid for themselves. The agreements also saved regulators time and money while meeting the needs of their comprehensive plans.

Example 3

Volvo: Strategic Goal-Setting and Target-Setting

The AB Volvo Environmental Board challenged its companies every year to set goals compatible with Volvo's broader strategic priorities on business, safety, and environmental performance. Once the individual companies set goals, the Corporate Environmental Board reviewed and compared them. This generated spirited competition among the companies that, tempered by corporate oversight, reinforced ownership and stimulated continuing improvement. Environmental specialists and other functions at Volvo Car Company worked together to set production and product goals for energy efficiency and fuel consumption, emissions in manufacturing and product use, recycling and waste management, and sustainability. Volvo set a clear target for each goal and tracked progress against the target. Each engineering department—e.g., exterior, body, chassis, engine, transmission, styling, interior—used these targets to develop its investment strategy. Each product design team used these targets to set performance and cost goals for new products. This approach allowed Volvo decisionmakers throughout the company to look beyond environmental regulations to understand how their decisions related to broader strategic goals in Volvo.

RAND's analysis indicates that the proactive firms conducting these experiments have used nine devices to integrate environmental concerns more effectively into core corporate activities, as the following sections describe.

IDENTIFY STAKEHOLDERS AND RELATED GOALS

The firm identifies its key stakeholders and clarifies its goals with respect to each of these stakeholders. The stakeholders commercial firms mention most often include customers, employees, shareholders, and the external community, including regulators. Any corporate culture is shaped and tested to serve a specific constellation of interests. A desire to integrate environmental concerns with the core concerns of the firm is typically a recognition that a firm's constellation of stakeholders or of their interests has shifted and that the firm must accommodate this shift for the firm to remain viable and successful. For example, customers may demand "greener" products; regulators may offer incentives for becoming more proactive; employees and local communities may become increasingly fearful

Example 4

Procter & Gamble: Community Interview Program

P&G's Mehoopany plant conducted in-depth interviews with community stakeholders on their views about the plant. Interviews covered employees from the community, others randomly chosen on the telephone, and "thought leaders" in the local community— environmental leaders, regulators, teachers, newspaper editors, health professionals, and leaders from other businesses. These interviews gave the plant a good picture of its local image, including any indications of concern. They allowed plant staff to meet face to face with many important external players, promoting a dialogue that could proceed without the pressure imposed by an immediate, specific decision or crisis. And they gave the nonenvironmental plant personnel who helped conduct these interviews a more-personal understanding of how environmental concerns in the community affected their core interests inside the plant.

of the effects of chemicals used in a plant; or shareholders may grow intolerant of the growing risk they associate with potential future regulation. Once the new constellation is accepted throughout the firm, the firm can then adjust its standard management practices to balance the interests of its stakeholders in a new way. The more deeply the firm can integrate the environmental concerns of its stakeholders into its normal management practices, the greater the firm's opportunity to achieve a cost-effective accommodation.

MAINTAIN SENIOR LEADERSHIP SUPPORT

Senior leadership in a firm takes responsibility for improved environmental management and promotes it as an issue of highest concern within the firm. Leadership has done this by making environmental performance part of the corporate vision statement or of a short list of high-level corporate goals; integrating environmental with health and safety functions; making the senior management position responsible for environmental, health, and safety functions a high-ranking corporate executive position that high-quality managers might strive for through their careers; and most important, personally participating in the development and promulgation of corporate environmental goals and the periodic review of corporate performance relative to these goals. All these actions bring environmental concerns closer to the core interest of the firm and thereby raise the credibility of the actions in the eyes of all employees.

Example 5

Volvo: Environmental Competency Center

Volvo Car Company's Environmental Competency Center was part of its Strategy and Business Development organization, which was broadly responsible for property development, product planning, customer software and hardware development, marketing, and target market decisions. The center's staff affected decisions in Volvo only by persuading others to act. It recommended corporate environmental policies for higher-level consideration. It affected product design by persuading individual product design teams to consider environmental effects in their designs. To do this, a group of experts on all phases of auto life—development, production, use, and recycling—worked with environmental coordinators to develop goals and strategies for the company and its business units. Placing this center at a single high level within Volvo provided the basis for a critical mass important to effective mutual support and information sharing.

Example 6

Hewlett-Packard: Strategic Metrics for Decisionmaking

HP used a common set of strategic metrics to guide all its decisions, from managing and rewarding employees, to designing products, to choosing suppliers. "TQRDC-E" summarized this system: technology, quality, responsiveness, delivery, cost, and environment. Environment was the most recent addition to the list. Giving environmental concerns such a high profile among its goals helped HP drive environmental considerations into decisions throughout the organization.

GIVE ENVIRONMENTAL CHAMPIONS DAY-TO-DAY RESPONSIBILITY

Senior leadership cannot spend all its time on any one issue but must appoint executives and managers who can work full time on environmental issues and act in the leadership's name on a day-to-day basis. Such "champions" are held accountable for the success of the organization's environmental program. Their primary job is to protect and promote broad corporate goals as the specialists responsible for implementation spell out the day-to-day details of the corporate environmental policy. That is, even as environmental goals become more important to the firm, they do not become all

Example 7

Hewlett-Packard: Environmental Stewardship Program

HP's environmental stewardship program in effect built an entire corporate environmental policy around champions strategically placed throughout a highly decentralized and entrepreneurial organization. Each business and product line had a steward. This placed 75 to 100 environmental champions in normal business processes—research and development (R&D), marketing, manufacturing, procurement, distribution, and especially design—around the world. Stewards established policies and tools supporting environmental policy implementation for the business overall. They communicated to raise awareness; tracked, assessed, and related market and legislative trends to HP strategic goals; advocated new procedures to reflect environmental priorities in corporate decisions; and deployed metrics and other tools to support decisionmaking. In each product line, stewards effectively linked environmental issues to design teams. To ensure that they were effective where they worked, HP chose stewards for their experience in R&D, manufacturing, or marketing as often as it did for their environmental experience. HP valued salesmanship, enthusiasm, aggressiveness, and influence in these stewards, who could affect corporate outcomes primarily by persuading others in HP that environmental concerns were important to HP's strategic goals and corporate performance.

important; champions must find and maintain the right balance in terms of day-to-day decisions.

Such champions are most likely to succeed if they come from the traditional management track in the company and are not environmental specialists themselves. They must be experienced enough as managers to ensure that they can induce others with specialized skills to perform for them. Inevitably, they become advocates for the specific proposals that their subordinates develop, but they must find ways to temper and then promote the proposals in ways that reflect the broader goals of the organization.

As the linchpins in the middle of this integration process, the firm's environmental champions must succeed for integration to be effective. Success depends on a firm's being able to draw high-quality, experienced general managers into these positions. That means the positions must have status as desirable locations on a promotion path in the firm.

BUILD COALITIONS WITH OTHER INTERNAL INTERESTS

Just as the notion of integration points to the presence of stakeholders with multiple interests in the firm, it also points to the importance of power within the firm and the need to build coalitions among interest groups to give environmental concerns appropriate weight in corporate decisionmaking.

Coalition-building is easier when environmental managers can state their goals in terms relevant to others in the firm. When a firm's customers seek "green" products, marketing becomes a natural ally for the environmental function. When environmental emissions account for a significant portion of operating costs, those responsible for cutting operating costs, through reengineering, quality programs, or other methods, become natural allies.

Broader coalitions make it easier to see environmental concerns as compatible with core organizational concerns, thereby raising their legitimacy throughout the organization. Higher legitimacy should make environmental concerns more successful in intracorporate negotiations and draw more-effective corporate personnel to activities responsible for environmental decisionmaking.

Example 8

WDWR: Cost Savings Through "Environmentality"

Cost savings were an important part of WDWR's "Environmentality" program. Pollution-prevention investments, for example, had to be justified by cost savings. When Environmental Initiatives, which coordinated environmental issues at WDWR, approached Disney properties with environmental proposals, its first question was "How would you like to save some money?" Environmental Initiatives compiled 20 money-saving examples to show the properties. It could offer clear financial arguments, for example, based on WDWR's own recent experience, that recycling and using recycled materials cut total ownership costs. Some of the examples of activities that were both better for the environment and saved money included using recycled laser printer cartridges instead of buying new ones, using hardwood mulch instead of cypress, making duplex instead of single-sided copies, composting food waste instead of sending it to a landfill, and using "green" lighting. These data benchmarked properties at WDWR relative to one another, promoting a friendly kind of competition to improve.

INTEGRATE RELEVANT ELEMENTS OF THE VALUE CHAIN

An organization can rarely serve its customers' needs by itself. It normally buys goods and services from other organizations to use in its own production activities or coordinates them with external partners also serving its customers. A "value chain" for each product delivered to an ultimate customer identifies each activity that contributes to the provision of that product. The environmental performance of the total value chain depends on environmental management in each link of the chain. Even if each organization in a value chain creates the coalitions needed to integrate environmental concerns with the core concerns of its own organization, still-broader coalitions that reach across organizations can improve such integration throughout the value chain.

Organizations must first decide which environmental activities to keep in house and which to coordinate with external sources. The decision typically depends on an organization's general willingness to depend on external sources. Organizations generally prefer to

Example 9

DuPont and Olin: Views on Internal and External Sources

Because DuPont and Olin had different broad corporate views of outsourcing, they took different approaches to the use of external sources to support their remediation efforts. DuPont was uncomfortable using external sources. For example, it retained responsibility in house for designing the rail cars it uses to transport hazardous chemicals. So it is not surprising that it maintained its own in-house DuPont Environmental Remediation Services to produce design and construction services. Olin's routine use of external sources to process bulk chemicals made it much more comfortable with outsourcing. It relied heavily on contractors for legal, design, analysis, assessment, and construction services. It developed careful arrangements to limit the liability that external sources might present. Olin maintained short lists of preferred providers for remediation services and planned to shorten the list so that it could develop closer relationships with a few strategic partners. It chose these providers carefully, even considering their relationships with regional Environmental Protection Agency (EPA) offices. Olin preferred on-site disposal, but gave special attention to off-site providers. To discourage use of many of these, Olin was considering financial incentives to charge business units for using such disposal.

Example 10

IBM and Ford: Views on Using ISO 14001 to Qualify Suppliers

IBM encouraged its suppliers to align their environmental management systems to ISO 14001 and to pursue registration to the standard. Arguing from the perspective of an integrated supply chain, IBM expected ISO 14001 to improve the efficiency and effectiveness of its suppliers. Within an integrated supply chain, IBM could naturally expect some of the benefits to accrue to itself. That possibility aside, IBM reserved the right to require such registration in the future. If the image of an "environmentally responsible supplier" came to include registration to ISO 14001, it would be natural for IBM to expect its suppliers to register. In contrast, Ford planned to focus on full implementation of QS-9000, the automobile industry version of ISO 9000, among its suppliers before it gave serious attention to ISO 14001 in this context.

retain activities that present higher risks, such as disposal of hazardous wastes that can potentially bring joint and several liability. The better the arrangements for managing relationships with external sources, the more willing firms are to rely on external sources.

Organizations tend to seek partners for the value chains in which they operate that share common environmental goals. Proactive organizations, then, typically include criteria in their source-selection processes that favor proactive suppliers. Proactive organizations also attempt to improve the performance of the partners

Example 11

Procter & Gamble: Influencing Suppliers' Environmental Performance

Significant environmental impacts relevant to P&G's paper manufacturing were linked to its suppliers. Even though P&G's Mehoopany plant owned no forests, it promoted sustainable forestry to protect the local hardwood forests that it relied upon to ensure the continuing availability and quality of its pulp. It gave its suppliers technical environmental and safety training. It reached agreements with suppliers to avoid logging during the muddy "breakup" periods during the spring and fall, when logging operations can especially damage the forests. Mehoopany was close to requiring its suppliers to use certain green and safe practices as part of a broader effort to address quality, safety, and environmental issues in the supplier qualification process.

they choose by providing training and technical assistance, sharing databases, and working together to develop new tools, processes, and practices. Such cooperation is not altruistic and can often involve hard bargaining and negotiation over how to share the gains from cooperation. By helping integrate the value chain, such activities reduce each participant's cost of achieving any given environmental goal for the internal processes it uses and the products that it offers.

STATE ENVIRONMENTAL GOALS IN SIMPLE, SPECIFIC TERMS

Integration inevitably leads to renegotiation among the interests inside and outside the firm. That negotiation will be most fruitful if it can generate environmental goals that the firm can state in simple, specific, concrete terms that allow individual decisionmakers in the firm to make decisions without further negotiation among interests. Such goals do not end the negotiation. They simply limit it to cases that cannot be governed by a few simple rules.

For example, the goal of ensuring compliance with all current laws is simpler to state and use than any goal about the importance of pollution prevention. Any goal referencing pollution prevention must provide a way to think about what a manager should be willing to

Example 12

Ford: Environmental Performance Targets in the Business Plan

Ford identified the following simple, clear, concrete, quantitative environmental performance targets to include in its 1998 Manufacturing Business Plan:

1.   certify all manufacturing plants worldwide to ISO 14001 by the end of 1998

2.   use 90 percent of returnable containers in facilities by 2001

3.   reduce paint shop emissions by 60 g/m^2 by 2005

4.   phase out all polychlorinated biphenyl (PCB) transformers by 2010

5.   reduce energy usage by 1 percent per year.

Each plant had its own, additional, clearly stated objectives and targets. The Ford Environmental System tracked each of these goals, year by year.

Example 13

Procter & Gamble: Allocating Environmental Costs

P&G allocated environmental costs to the business units responsible for generating these costs. At its Mehoopany plant, for example, it placed all environmentally related costs in well-defined cost pools, developed simple rules and supporting practices to allocate each pool to a product module, and gave its Mehoopany Environmental Group—the cross-functional department with primary environmental responsibility for promoting and integrating environmental activities throughout the plant—authority to oversee and enforce this accounting system. The system worked well. For example, it tracked all waste streams and either charged business modules for costs imposed by waste or credited them for revenues generated by selling waste or cost displaced by using waste in in-house processes. Fuel displaced was valued at the full cost savings associated with the fuel. To allocate the cost of all solid waste passing through the single transport point on the way to disposal, Mehoopany simply weighed each container coming from a product module to the transport point and allocated cost in proportion to weight. This allocation was not exactly right, but close enough. A central corporate fund not allocated to product modules covered most Superfund remediation costs.

sacrifice with regard to the core interests of the firm to invest in pollution prevention that goes beyond compliance. A common "win-win" answer is that pollution prevention is appropriate where full environmental accounting reveals that it is cost-effective for the firm; in effect, the goal becomes the use of more-comprehensive cost-benefit analysis, which must then be defined.

USE CROSS-FUNCTIONAL TEAMS FOR SPECIFIC DECISIONS, PROJECTS, AND PROCESSES

At the level of specific decisions, projects, or processes, cross-functional teams provide a way to bring an environmental perspective into corporate decisions and to temper the environmental perspective with broader corporate concerns. Simply placing a functional interest on a team does not mean the team will reflect the interests of that functional area. The legitimacy of environmental concerns to broad corporate interests must be clearly established before members of the team will take the environmental member seriously.

Example 14

DuPont: Corporate Remediation Group

DuPont's Corporate Remediation Group brought together staff formerly located in its Legal and Engineering Departments with staff from individual remediation sites. This new group included cross-functional skills in program management, remediation technologies, and remediation regulations. DuPont's senior leadership expected this structure to focus remediation policies and actions more clearly on DuPont's strategic goals, provide uniform policies throughout the company and effective accountability for their implementation, integrate the disciplines that DuPont had available to address remediation, track total remediation-related costs more effectively and make them more visible, take more-effective advantage of advice from contractors, and improve communication of lessons learned on best practices. As the leadership had also expected, such a central organization helped effect what the leaders considered to be a major change in organizational direction.

Cross-functional teams are most effective when their members are authorized to make decisions in their functions' names and not simply to represent their functions' positions without decisionmaking authority. This typically means that the environmental specialists serving on such teams should have broad capabilities within their environmental specialty. Such capabilities are most effective when the environmental function allows effective training over the course of an individual's career. That is, heavy use of cross-functional teams should not so overwhelm the participants' time

Example 15

Olin: Team-Based Decisionmaking

After successfully moving to team-based decisionmaking in other parts of its organization, Olin implemented cross-functional team-based decisionmaking in remediation. Team-based decisionmaking became the foundation of Olin's remediation management system. This approach emphasized processes over functions. Olin supported this effort with training on consensus-based decisionmaking and conflict resolution. It then used detailed metrics to track the performance of each team and based a significant portion of team members' pay on the performance of the teams on which they participated. Olin found that a small number of employees could not adapt to this new approach and had to release them.

that they cannot develop or maintain competence in the functions they are supposed to bring to a team.

Teams work best when governed by consensus and, with experience, team members tend to develop skills that support consensus decisionmaking. But to the extent that teams require leaders or that leaders need to intervene to manage a failure to reach consensus, the leaders come from a broad management background, not a functional specialty, such as environment.

DEVELOP TOOLS TO IDENTIFY FIRMWIDE EFFECTS OF ENVIRONMENTALLY RELATED ACTIVITIES

Cross-functional teams have traditionally represented all parts of the firm affected by the decision, project, or process the team owns; the use of such teams is a formal recognition that "externalities" exist even within firms and that some form of integration is required to internalize these externalities within the firm.[2] Teams bring diverse experiences and skills to bear on questions to manage problems.

Externalities can also be identified for management with information systems that capture the effects of a decision throughout a firm, now

Example 16

Volvo: Environmental Priorities Strategies System

Volvo's Environmental Priorities Strategies system comprised a methodology and database that together provided decision support for designers. It could reduce very complex information, if desired, to a single number that designers could use to support specific design decisions. It established goals for life-cycle analysis, documented an inventory of life-cycle environmental impacts, measured the effects of these impacts on human health and the environment, and calculated a single number that designers could use to support trade-offs. These designers could apply the system quickly and easily to weigh alternatives.

---

[2]An *externality* exists in a particular setting when the outcome of the decision can affect people not represented in the decision. The most common way to correct this problem is to find ways to inject the interests of the missing parties into the decision, either by ensuring their direct participation, or by injecting taxes, subsidies, or controls designed to reflect their missing interests.

Example 17

Hewlett-Packard: Environmental Database

HP's Fountainhead environmental database provided information relevant to contacts, policy and business issues, specific application areas within HP for environmental policy business groups and regions relevant to HP, recommendations on compliance strategies and corporate policies, and breaking news. Over 50,000 staff members in HP's many decentralized business units used Fountainhead for decision support.

and in the future. Information systems and analytic tools that identify the full, firmwide effects of environmentally related activities are essential to effective integration of the environmental and core interests of the firm. Examples are (1) life-cycle assessment, which identifies the effects during operation and support of a system of its initial design, and (2) activity-based costing, which fully attributes environmental compliance costs to decisions about the design and operation of a firm's core production processes. These tools use what is in effect a traditional cash-flow approach to costing, but one more comprehensive and inclusive with regard to the costs (and benefits) included in the analysis.

BALANCE CENTRALIZATION AND DECENTRALIZATION

Efforts to integrate environmental and core concerns naturally raise questions about how centralized environmental activities should be. Effective commercial firms choose an appropriate balance of centralization and decentralization.

To promote integration with core activities, these firms seek to decentralize environmental activities to the same extent that they decentralize their core activities. Core activity managers take responsibility for environmental issues relevant to their core activities. To allow this, proactive firms typically decentralize management of environmental activities relevant to the products produced at particular sites. Such decentralized management recognizes variation in product-level priorities and in regulatory environments across the firm. To reflect such variation, these firms attribute the costs associated with site-specific environmental activities to the appropriate products. They weigh and manage compliance and pollution prevention options locally and manage the permitting processes relevant to these products locally.

Proactive firms centralize environmental activities only if they are not closely related to their core activities or if a uniform corporate environmental practice is cost-effective. The segregation of certain remediation activities in a centrally managed business unit is a commonly observed example of the first kind. Remediation of sites used for disposal in the past is not directly related to current product design or production decisions. Examples of the second kind are lists of preferred providers of disposal, treatment, and recycling services. These are often centrally managed to simplify corporate oversight of the providers, to limit total corporate liability exposure, and to enhance corporate bargaining power when negotiating prices for these services.

Auditing functions often reflect a mix: They draw on centralized data systems compatible with the corporate information architecture but draw auditors from throughout the corporation to enhance transfer of lessons learned between divisions. Such cross-divisional management promotes the goal of integrating the efforts of all parts of the organization to coordinate environmental and core concerns cost-effectively. Decentralized management allows what are in effect many experiments; centralized auditing helps the whole organization benefit from these experiments.

Example 18

DuPont and Olin: Centralized Remediation Programs

DuPont and Olin sought to place financial and management responsibility with the business unit that creates a problem. When relevant state and local regulations varied, it was often better to place relevant responsibilities with local units. But this had to be balanced with the visibility and control of costs and funding and the consistent application of policy that central assignment of responsibility supports. On balance, DuPont and Olin chose to centralize remediation responsibilities. Taking responsibility away from the active product units allowed them to focus on environmental issues relevant to current and future production. That said, to ensure that its 19 individual business units maintained some awareness that remediation costs money, DuPont taxed these business units to cover 35 percent of ongoing remediation costs.

IMPLICATIONS FOR DOD

Broadly speaking, as noted above, OSD's formal policies on environmental management are consistent with the major policy points made above. Drawing on our survey of private-sector experience, we believe that the real benefit that OSD can gain from best commercial practice comes from its experience with implementing proactive environmental management policy. Implementation includes the details of how an organization fleshes out the policy points above; OSD may benefit from some of the details of policy design discussed above. The real challenge associated with implementation involves broader questions about managing change in a large organization. We turn to that challenge in the following chapter. As we shall see, at a high level, OSD advocates many of the general points but is still working to use these points to translate its policy into day-to-day practice in DoD.

CENTRAL IMPLEMENTATION CHALLENGE 1: THERE ARE NO SILVER BULLETS WHEN EVERY SITUATION IS DIFFERENT

RAND's literature review and case study research indicate that, when a firm succeeds in integrating its environmental and core management concerns, the implementation of environmental management policy becomes an integral part of day-to-day management. Successful implementation is then no more or less than successful management. Successful managers, of course, will tell you that few tasks are more challenging. The way successful commercial firms remunerate their successful managers confirms this: They are highly valued employees. Commercial firms that have succeeded in implementing new approaches to environmental management all talk about how important the basics of good management practices are to their success. These practices typically involve a much broader range of issues than environmental management per se and must be

Example 19

Volvo: Views on Affecting Automobile Environmental Performance

Volvo found that environmental issues play a part in roughly 35 overall attributes relevant to the design of an automobile—for example, weight, air resistance, and rolling resistance. These issues were the only concerns relevant to emission and recycling rates; they were very important to the consideration of materials and fuel consumption. Volvo could ensure that its automobile designs properly reflected corporate environmental concerns only by directly affecting the decisions of the individual designers who chose the values of attributes in any new design. Success lay entirely in affecting individual or team decisions.

embedded in the general management practices of the organization.[1]

MOTIVATE CREATIVE AND PERSISTENT CHANGE AGENTS

A successfully implemented environmental management system motivates managers and other employees to approach environmentally related decisions as creative and persistent change agents. In most firms, the standard way of executing core activities within the firm has not traditionally given explicit attention to environmental concerns. And the standard relationship between a firm and its regulators has not created a great deal of room for mutually beneficial discussion, much less negotiation. Any effort at change creates resistance. Alternatives to the status quo can threaten people with a vested interest in the current way of doing business, both inside and outside the organization. Even environmental specialists who have become experts on managing end-of-pipe solutions and traditional regulation can find a more-proactive approach that raises the visibility of environmental management very threatening.

Example 20

DuPont: Aligning Environmental Concerns with Business Priorities

At DuPont, aligning environmental concerns with business priorities meant bringing a traditional business perspective to bear on environmental issues. This perspective demands flexibility, creativity, innovation, and team-building to get things done. In particular, it does not view regulations as fixed in stone. Working from a clear set of goals on how to protect human health and the environment, DuPont sought cost-effective approaches to pursue these goals, even if current regulations did not immediately permit these approaches. DuPont relied on constant application of peer-reviewed science and careful management of its relationships with regulators to build its case and constantly question the status quo. The environmental champion coordinated this effort, which is why DuPont preferred a manager with an exemplary business background in a core product area, rather than an environmental specialist, to be the champion.

---

[1]For useful overviews of these implementation issues, see Bardach (1979), Williams (1980), Zellman (1993), and Kotter (1996).

Alternatives to the status quo may take time and effort to work as well as the status quo does or to achieve as much acceptance among customers. Proactive firms seek ways to overcome these problems at the front line of change itself, one manager at a time. Our research suggests that a creative manager is necessary but that creativity is not sufficient. Creativity can provide cost-effective alternatives to the status quo; persistence and motivation are necessary to see the alternatives through to ultimate adoption.[2]

ASSIGN RESPONSIBILITIES CLEARLY THROUGHOUT THE FIRM

It is tempting to reflect the goal of full integration in a statement that "environmental management is everyone's responsibility." Proactive firms find that anything that is everyone's responsibility is no one's responsibility; it easily falls through the cracks. Successful integration requires a clear assignment of responsibilities throughout the firm.

For example, firms may hold a centralized organization responsible for remediating closed disposal sites but charge operating divisions for any remediation associated with disposal after a date certain. Firms may charge operating divisions for compliance costs associated with their operations rather than covering them from corporate overhead.

At each level in the firm, general management is responsible for successful implementation of its environmental management system, but delegates day-to-day responsibility to a champion, whom general management then monitors on a regular basis. The champion "owns" environmental management but does not manage the production activities in which compliance and many pollution prevention activities actually occur. The champion informs her or his supervisors about such activities so that the supervisors can remain accountable for all aspects of production activities, including the environmental elements. Although this approach assigns responsibility clearly, it allows multiple channels of communication between

---

[2]For an excellent example of the kind of behavior desired, see Berube et al. (1992).

Example 21

WDWR: Environmental Responsibility at the Contemporary Hotel

In 1996, the principal environmental point of contact at the Contemporary Hotel at WDWR, with 1,050 rooms and 120,000 square feet of meeting space, was its operations manager. He was also the energy chairman. He personally spearheaded many environmental initiatives. He believed that "Environmentality"— Disney's proactive approach to environmental management—positively enhanced the guest experience and the hotel's use of resources, both close to his core concerns. The hotel recycled 59 percent of its waste stream, most of it cardboard, and all of its food waste. One simple initiative became a regularly anticipated part of the entertainment at the hotel. The hotel released ladybugs to help control aphids. To do this, a costumed cast member, named "Dr. L. Bug," gathered children in the back of the hotel and gave each child a small container of ladybugs. The children then released the ladybugs while their parents took pictures.

the leadership and the field. These channels and the authority associated with them must be repeatedly adjusted in response to actual performance to get the balance between environmental and core concerns that the leadership seeks.

DESIGN METRICS TO MOTIVATE THE RIGHT BEHAVIOR

We have seen that successful firms manage what can be measured. This cliché can be overstated, but proactive firms rely on metrics as the foundation for managing improvement. Accounting is often called the language of business. Metrics extend this notion more broadly to reflect the importance of nonmonetary, as well as monetary, measures of performance.

Although metrics can play many roles, the key role here is one of motivating behavior. Such "motivational" metrics measure a team or manager's success and provide a basis for allocating the net value added that the firm generates among units of the firm. This applies throughout the firm, from top to bottom. Metrics designed to motivate behavior must be carefully crafted for each decision setting throughout the firm to ensure that they (1) induce the decisionmaker to pursue firmwide goals, (2) are compatible with the constraints that the decisionmaker faces in each setting, (3) are easy to collect and verify, and (4) are mutually understood and accepted by the decisionmaker and oversight authority (Kaplan, 1990; Kaplan and Norton, 1996; Kaplan and Norton, 2000).

In practice, successful firms find that metrics that meet these criteria more nearly approximate firmwide goals as a decisionmaker has more discretion. Hence, metrics differ at different levels and locations in the firm. The firms also find that, at lower levels, such met-

Example 22

Olin: Metrics for Managing Remediation

As part of its broader quality-based management culture, Olin sought to use quantitative metrics to capture relevant business information about its remediation activities. Most important was economic value added, the standard measure of performance used throughout Olin, which Olin tracked in terms of cost avoidance, cost savings, and cost recovery associated with remediation activities. It also regularly tracked cost management, changes in spending projections, relationship management, public perceptions of Olin's remediation program, significant remediation accomplishments, extraordinary adverse effects, and performance at individual sites. To track relationship management, for example, Olin regularly administered short, formal questionnaires to key regulators and senior Olin leaders. When documenting remediation accomplishments, Olin sought the best estimates possible of their effects on economic value added. It tracked reports in the media for extraordinary adverse effects. Olin reported these metrics regularly to its senior leadership and used these metrics to calculate bonuses for its remediation personnel. In effect, Olin tried to manage remediation as much as possible like a profit center rather than a cost center.

Example 23

Hewlett-Packard: Guidelines for Developing Metrics

HP used the following guidelines to develop metrics:

1. They should be simple and easy to use.

2. They should be strategically relevant and empirically based on HP experience.

3. Product designers should be able to influence them.

4. They should provide a starting point, not a full-blown solution; they should mature with experience.

Example 24

Procter & Gamble: Key Element Assessment Audits

As part of broader quality-based practices, P&G conducted an annual Key Element Assessment audit at each plant. Such audits took three days to review environmental issues, three days to review safety issues, and additional time to review other quality issues. Personnel from one plant helped conduct audits at other plants to calculate metrics that each plant could use to measure its progress against its own past performance; such cross-plant audits helped transfer lessons learned across sites. The audits subjectively rated each site, using a scale of 1 to 10, on specific factors relevant to government and public relations (e.g., compliance, inspections, and community relationships), people capacity (e.g., leadership, training, accountability, and program support and expectations), direct environmental impact (e.g., monitoring emissions, assessment of waste management, and management of process change), incident prevention (e.g., prevention plan, special risk programs for specific chemicals on site, emergency response plans and training, and spill protection), and continuous improvement (e.g., audit frequency and follow-up, waste and cost reduction, goals and measurement progress, and reduction of complexity relevant to environmental effects).

rics must be adjusted continually over time in response to experience with them. This is true in part because individuals respond differently to similar incentives.

More importantly, quantitative metrics by themselves can rarely capture everything important about a decisionmaking position. Proactive firms typically supplement their quantitative metrics with qualitative metrics on the overall operation of important processes. They may also give their managers the discretion to adjust the quantitative metrics associated with particular options under consideration to reflect their subjective judgment about the cost-effectiveness of these options for the organization as a whole.

These considerations present a special challenge for environmental management. As noted above, integrating environmental management with other management concerns is about innovation. Metrics provide the basis not just for inducing everyone to execute the existing production process as well as possible but also to improve the production process continually to reduce the environmental damage associated with production. Innovative circumstances typically call for metrics that reflect an unconstrained work environment and hence that reflect the firm's goals as broadly as possible. But environmental management must ultimately be implemented in a constrained environment, with metrics that reflect this environment. The tension between unconstrained metrics aimed at innovation and constrained metrics that implement an innovation is not easy to resolve, especially when change is continuing.

In individual firms, we found that innovation is often driven by engineering groups affiliated with production but able to take a broader perspective. In these circumstances, the engineers can work with metrics closer to corporate environmental goals than would be appropriate for the workers on the production line. For example, the engineers might use metrics that reflect the companywide costs associated with using a chemical, while the workers on the line would use metrics that track their implementation of tighter housekeeping and pharmacy practices developed by the engineers. Such a distinction becomes more problematic in firms that rely more heavily on production teams themselves for innovation.

USE INCENTIVES TO MOTIVATE THE RIGHT BEHAVIOR

Metrics can motivate behavior only if linked to incentives. Every firm seeking to improve its environmental management gives special attention to incentives; they tend to choose incentives that are compatible with their prevailing corporate cultures. Depending on the culture, incentives target individuals, teams, or organizations. They can be direct or indirect, monetary or nonmonetary (Hoffman, 1992–93).

The most common form of incentive appears to be a direct, nonmonetary award to individuals who have tangibly improved environmental management. Firms emphasize the importance of giving such awards often, even for small improvements, to spread the importance of environmental management throughout the organization. Firms that offer bonuses for large improvements include environmental management in such programs. Other firms refuse to pay individual employees cash for "doing their job."

Many firms point to the importance of placing key environmental management positions on a promotion path that attracts highly qualified managers and rewards them for good performance with

Example 25

WDWR: Nonmonetary Incentives at WDWR

WDWR did not rely heavily on cash to reward most individuals or teams working at the location. The local culture supported other motivational devices. Environmental Initiatives, which coordinated environmental programs at WDWR, distributed a pin depicting Jiminy Cricket (a long-time favorite Disney character) to any cast member who participated in an environmental circle. It distributed silver and gold Environmental Excellence awards to members associated with outstanding environmental activities. These were among only three types of pins that cast members could attach to their name tags to highlight their achievements at Disney. In 1996, the Disney Corporate Vice President for Environmental Policy awarded the gold pins at an annual ceremony at Epcot Center on Earth Day. Also in 1996, employee groups at the Contemporary Hotel made six monthly awards to departments at the hotel for best and worst performer against environmental, energy, and safety and security goals. The recipients of the trophies, which rotated each month, had to display them prominently. The positive environmental trophy was a statue of Jiminy Cricket; the negative trophy was a rubber chicken in a noose.

promotions. Team-oriented firms can use formulas to allocate profit-sharing bonuses to team members; they can write these formulas to reflect environmental management activities. Less directly, some companies argue that cost-effective environmental management improves overall corporate profits and that all employees benefit through profit-sharing arrangements.

Some firms try to "internalize" relevant costs by allocating compliance costs to the overhead costs of business units before assessing unit profits; others tax business units for using external sources for disposal or recycling services not included on a preapproved list.

In all these areas, many firms use competition among business units to heighten the incentive effects of these options and to gather internal benchmarks that can be used to allocate incentive awards among units.

In sum, the experiences outlined above suggest that DoD, like all proactive firms, should recognize the importance of incentives to successful implementation of environmental management. And DoD, like all proactive firms, should use the specific incentives that it is most comfortable with in its cultural setting.

MANAGE FAILURES TO LIMIT DISINCENTIVES FOR RISK-TAKING

A special incentive issue that proactive firms recognize is the challenge of dealing with failed experiments associated with pollution prevention. Trial and error offer great potential in any learning organization and are especially important in efforts to refine changes in an ongoing production process. Systematic learning depends on a system that supports flexibility and tolerates the right kinds of mistakes (Ochsner, Chess, and Greenberg, 1995–96). The most important aspect of successful experimentation is to recognize that failure is part of the learning process. The term "failing forward"—that is, "creating forward momentum with the learning derived from failures"—usefully describes this process (Leonard-Barton, 1996, p. 119). Operationalizing this belief involves distinguishing between intelligent failure and unnecessary failure and setting up systems to learn from both.

Most proactive firms seem to understand this, but we found little insight about how, specifically, to implement such understanding in DoD. How big a failure is acceptable? How many failures are acceptable? Who should be held accountable for failure when so many things can contribute? What kinds of decision screens can reduce the probability of failure without unduly discouraging experimentation? What kind of safety net can limit the effects of failure? Corporate cultures typically encourage conservative decisionmaking, supported by standard information sources and appeals to standard operating procedures that make failure far less likely than any attempt to change standard operating procedures.

Implementation of the kind of change being discussed here raises questions about all these points until a new culture, more tolerant of an increased emphasis on environmental considerations, takes the place of the old. Until firms develop good answers to such questions, it remains unclear how best to mitigate disincentives to change.

EMPOWER EMPLOYEES WITH FORMAL TRAINING

Perhaps the most common error firms have made when trying to make a large cultural change is to adjust formal responsibilities and metrics without training employees about what they expect. Five types of formal training are important to improvements in environmental management:

1. A firm trying to raise the perceived relative importance of environmental concerns internally provides training about the general social importance of environmental issues and the role the firm can play in this broader setting. Such training often integrates factual presentations, emotional appeals, and open-discussion groups to try to change the attitudes or even the values of the firm's employees.

2. Firms using new management methods (such as cross-functional teams) to promote integration, train their employees in the use of these methods and in more-general consensus-building and problem-solving techniques relevant to the success of such teams. Similar training is important to any manager being asked to be more creative and persistent about environmental issues, although general management experience is often the best teacher of these skills.

3. Firms seeking to develop environmental specialists who can operate confidently in many aspects of environmental decision-making—for example, specialists who can function effectively as decisionmakers on cross-functional teams—develop databases that these employees can use for self-paced instruction. Such databases offer current information on technologies or case studies of past decisions that young employees can access as needed when they face specific problems in their day-to-day work.

Example 26
Volvo: Environmental Training Program

Volvo believed it necessary to change attitudes to promote improved environmental performance for its products. It used a program called Volvo Dialogue to train all employees, dealers, and suppliers worldwide. Training occurred in stages, starting in house in Sweden and moving out. Session 1 scared and shocked attendees to get their attention. In Session 2, a Volvo employee trained his or her colleagues on how transportation affects the environment worldwide. In Session 3, a Volvo employee finally trained attendees on Volvo's role in the environment. Volvo monitored progress and had empirical evidence that this training program, the largest in its history, was achieving the results sought.

Example 27

DuPont: Remediation Information System

DuPont used Having Everything About Remediation Technologies (HEART), a CD-ROM-based information system and technical library, to make technical and legal information available to all relevant players, especially junior staff just learning about remediation. HEART included information on technology initiatives, costs, regulations, where DuPont had implemented specific technologies, and references to the open literatures. It included logic trees and selection matrices that supported decisions on choosing remediation technologies for specific sites. These CD-ROMs contained a great deal of proprietary and sensitive material and were appropriately controlled. DuPont updated the CD-ROMs periodically.

4. Firms facing new regulations, introducing new pollution prevention programs, or adopting new databases or analytic tools offer targeted training to the employees that these changes will affect most directly.

5. Firms seeking to establish a critical mass of expertise on environmental issues, which can sustain their experts over time and help them work together to keep their skills up to date, form centers of excellence or competence centers. Such centers can support the training options listed above and provide points of focus for longer-term career development.

In all of this, we note that training takes time. Formal training is more time intensive, the more interaction the firm seeks between trainer and trainee. Over the longer term, informal on-the-job training related to the execution of new programs and procedures continues indefinitely.

DEVELOP A SUPPORTIVE ORGANIZATIONAL CONTEXT FOR TOOLS

Improved tools can enhance environmental management in DoD. We encountered such salient, desirable tools as

1. environmental audits

2. resource, energy, and material tracking systems

3. accounting systems that link environmental effects to various decisions

4. engineering models of core production and remediation activities that help firms compare the effects of alternative environmental actions.

Unfortunately, even when these tools are available, they tend to have limited capabilities.

To date, audits have offered commercial firms the most powerful tools. The federal regulatory program that introduced the Toxic Release Inventory in 1987 can be viewed as a management auditing tool, even if it was externally imposed.[3] The visibility its simple quantitative reports offer has had a profound effect on how companies think about the relative importance of environmental management. Internal audits that offer much-more-extensive visibility within a firm have also helped the senior leadership of firms appreciate the pervasiveness of environmental effects in their core activities.[4] Information from such audits has been instrumental in jolting the senior leaders of now-proactive firms into a proactive stance.

Example 28

Hewlett-Packard: Developing Life-Cycle Assessment Tools

HP did not attempt to conduct full-blown life-cycle analyses of all environmental impacts relevant to design decisions. Rather, it focused its efforts where they were likely to have the largest payoffs. It worked through the product value chain and life cycle, from R&D to disposal, and performed gross assessments of environmental impacts. This approach provided a basis for broad, generic design-for-environment guidelines on packaging, consumables and supplies, manufacturing processes, and end-of-life strategy that decisionmakers could apply to all products. For example, guidelines sought to reduce mass, eliminate hazardous materials, and reduce the number of components in a design. This effort drew directly on recycling and reuse experience gained at HP's recovery facilities in Roseville, California, and Grenoble, France.

---

[3]Superfund Amendments and Reauthorization Act (1986), Sec. 313.

[4]For an overview of auditing options, see Willig (1995).

Example 29

Volvo: Developing the Environmental Priorities Strategies System

Volvo's Environmental Priorities Strategies system evolved over time. Volvo began by using a simple version of it to support real decisions. As the system demonstrated its value, development proceeded. Volvo expected it to become increasingly sophisticated and useful as it matured in the course of use in real settings.

Such accounting systems as life-cycle assessment, "green" accounting, and activity-based costing remain primitive. Firms typically rely on existing cost accounts and draw the information needed to support specific decisions from these accounts as needed. Such analysis typically requires considerable discretion and judgment.

Engineering models have proven to be quite helpful in remediation when firms have learned to use them to support "win-win" negotiation with regulators. The effectiveness of using models of core production processes in environmental management depends heavily on how well production engineers knowledgeable about core activities integrate environmental and core concerns.

Ultimately, organizational concerns tend to dominate tool development; until a firm organizes itself in a way that allows it to use a tool effectively, the political support for tool development will be limited. That said, objective tools can provide DoD with the single strongest basis for shifting organizational attention toward environmental concerns.

COMMUNICATE CONTINUOUSLY IN ALL DIRECTIONS

Based on our analysis, all proactive firms agree that continuous communication, in all directions, about the goals and status of the environmental management program is important to success. Such communication serves five goals:

1. It conveys the senior leadership's commitment to effective environmental management to the whole organization. This occurs when the firm moves toward a new commitment to environmental management and then occurs repeatedly over time to verify continuing support.

2. It conveys knowledge about the realized performance of environmental management to the senior leadership so that it remains accountable for the environmental performance of the firm as a whole and so that it can make adjustments as needed to ensure that the environmental management program actually being implemented in the firm continues to reflect its corporatewide goals. Not incidentally, such communication maintains the awareness of senior leaders, contributing to their continuing willingness to support environmental management efforts in the broader context of the leadership's responsibilities.

3. It conveys information on successes from one business unit to another to maintain the momentum of change and to support learning across the organization. It conveys information about failures with similar goals in mind. Failures can threaten the program, especially early in its life, if the firm does not react to them constructively. Communication about failures is most successful when it also communicates a constructive corporate response.

4. It conveys information on the goals and status of the program to key stakeholders outside the firm. Communication with these groups reflects a firm's views of each group. Depending on its corporate vision, it can give special attention to customers, regulators, nongovernmental organizations, or local communities, including its employees who live there.

5. It promotes active exchange of information with the scientific community and national environmental groups. The latest information from the external scientific and policy community supports a firm's pursuit of creative solutions. Participation in the broader debate on environmental issues helps shape the direction of ongoing scientific research and regulatory reform.

MANAGE RELATIONSHIPS WITH STAKEHOLDERS

Continuing communication with external stakeholders is only one part of a broader program of managing relationships with these stakeholders effectively.

If a household acting as a customer is a key stakeholder, a firm may place special emphasis on building an "environmental profile" that differentiates its product from alternatives to maintain the loyalty of

Example 30

Olin: Relationships with External Stakeholders

Olin sought to engage its external stakeholders in normal times so that it could get their support when it needed it. Senior Olin officials held regular meetings with relevant EPA regional deputy administrators and maintained contact with other high-level regulators. Olin actually surveyed these regulators to monitor their views of Olin's performance. At the local level, Olin encouraged formation of community advisory panels. Olin contributed one participant to each panel and helped communities form and manage panels that could then give Olin community input at each site, sometimes with the help of a professional facilitator. It used these panels to avoid surprises, develop long-term relationships, and convey technical information.

buyers who prefer "green" products. This means building an objective case that it is sufficiently clean and communicating this case in language that the customer will understand and accept. Formal eco-labeling programs, where available, support this effort.[5] Communicating with external stakeholders also means communicating effectively with customers to understand what elements of environmental performance they value most.

If the customer is another company, the firm may well seek formal certification by a third party to verify that its environmental management practices meet the customer's needs.[6] If a regulator, local community, or nongovernmental organization is a key stakeholder, the firm places a high priority on gaining and maintaining the stakeholder's trust, respect, and good will. Trust provides a basis for mutually attractive information exchange and negotiation. An important part of this information exchange is information the firm hopes will train the stakeholder about specific elements of the firm's situation and goals.

Such training and risk communication can be critical when, as is often the case, the stakeholder is not as technically sophisticated as the firm itself. Stakeholders typically respond constructively to such

---

[5]See, for example, Kirchenstein and Jump (1995).

[6]For a useful discussion of available options, see Jackson (1995).

Example 31

Procter & Gamble: Relationships with External Stakeholders

P&G invested significant time in regulator relationships. Because state regulator personnel were often junior and inexperienced, particularly with regard to specific industrial processes, P&G trained state regulators on environmental issues relevant to its industry. Its plant at Mehoopany gave Pennsylvania Department of Environmental Protection employees tours of its facilities to demonstrate good environmental practices. Mehoopany personnel participated regularly in statewide forums on environmental issues, like the Air Quality Technical Advisory Committee and the Pennsylvania Governor's Twenty-First Century Environmental Commission, a panel of about 50 environmental groups, firms, government representatives, educators, and consulting firms asking how environmental issues should evolve in Pennsylvania in the 21st century.

Example 32

WDWR: Working with External Stakeholders on the 20-Year Permit

Disney worked closely with regulators and environmental groups to develop and finalize its 20-year permitting agreement at WDWR. Disney mapped all 31,000 acres of the site using a geographical information system. This mapping included hydrology, soils, wetlands, flora and fauna, endangered species, roads, and so on. Disney used this information to build an empirically based explanation of how the agreement would improve the environment and reduce regulator costs. From the beginning, Disney emphasized contact with local officials and groups. It also worked with regional and local EPA administrators and interested environmental and citizen groups. It adjusted its plan to reflect their suggestions. It set clear priorities on which wetlands to protect. Disney worked especially hard to avoid surprises. Over time, Disney's empirical arguments, its efforts to be honest and forthcoming, and the substance of its arguments convinced previously dubious players to trust Disney and proceed with the agreement.

training, of course, only if trust has already been established. Whoever the stakeholder is, these considerations encourage the firm to invest in its relationship with the stakeholder, seeking dialogue even when the firm is not seeking to sell a specific product or debating point.

Building trust and respect by nurturing a relationship is not the same as acquiescing to a stakeholder's demands. Managing stakeholders is always about balancing the interests of all stakeholders. A proactive firm seeks an open, frank exchange with each stakeholder that clearly articulates the basis for the firm's position with that stakeholder. Being open often facilitates discussion that leads to a mutually satisfactory outcome. But each stakeholder must understand that the firm respects all its stakeholders' needs and reflects them, in good faith, in its discussions with each individual stakeholder.

BENCHMARK TO PROMOTE CONTINUOUS IMPROVEMENT

Since 1985, proactive firms have turned increasingly to benchmarking to improve their performance. Benchmarking means different things to different firms. It can range from broad insights about another firm's performance level to very detailed studies in which the firm's specialists on a particular task compare notes with their counterparts in another firm and develop specific ways to adapt practices observed for application at home. But the key to benchmarking is a recognition that other firms have discovered solutions that any particular firm has not even dreamed of. And as innovation proceeds, other firms are bound to discover new solutions faster than any particular firm does.

Benchmarking to discover such solutions is as important to environmental management as it is to any other aspect of management. In some ways, benchmarking offers higher payoffs in environmental management because it is often possible to learn a great deal from the environmental management practices of firms in other industries—firms that are not competitors and are hence more likely to share sensitive information about innovative programs. Over the long run, repeated benchmarking offers standards against which firms can judge themselves and which these firms can use to adjust their goals repeatedly to pursue continuous improvement within their own organizations. Innovative firms have set up organizations like the Global Environmental Management Initiative (GEMI) to do precisely this in the field of environmental management.[7] Such consulting groups as A. D. Little, Arthur Andersen, and the American

---

[7]See, for example, GEMI (1994).

Productivity and Quality Center maintain more or less formal databases on best environmental management practices that they continually update to serve customers of their consulting practices.[8]

---

[8]See, for example, Blumenfeld and Montrone (1995), the Global Best Practices links at http://www.arthurandersen.com, and the International Benchmarking Clearinghouse links at http://www.apqc.org.

Chapter Five

CENTRAL IMPLEMENTATION CHALLENGE 2: RADICAL ORGANIZATIONAL CHANGE TAKES A LONG TIME

Any attempt to induce a major change in an organization as large as DoD takes time, the issue we tackle in this chapter.

A case for change must be built to take to the senior leadership. Following leadership signoff, teams must be formed to articulate policy and then transform it into specific, implementable actions. This often requires experimentation and prototyping to test the new policy in a way that limits the effects of failure. More often than not, more than one effort is required to create an implementable action that works as intended. Failure often results more from an unwillingness to accept the change in the organization than from any inherent flaw in the change itself. Often, the effort to achieve implementable change raises unexpected questions that need to be resolved at senior levels before work can proceed. Such questions often arise when the importance of activities not originally involved in the change becomes apparent only after implementation starts. Their role in the change must then be brokered, often at a high enough level to encompass all the affected offices.

These problems are not unmanageable. On the contrary, this general pattern of problems is quite predictable and manageable in fairly routine ways when organizations have become used to such changes. These organizations often have many such changes under way simultaneously in different parts of the organization. They break change down into manageable units and test one set of changes before going on to the next. Over time, change never ends in a learning organization but becomes a normal part of standard operating procedures.

Nonetheless, such organizations recognize that change takes time and that it requires more time as an action affects larger parts of the organization. Specific changes affecting small parts of an organization—say, a few hundred people—may take two years to work through. Implementing a specific change throughout an organization with tens of thousands of employees, such as DoD, can easily take five years or more. Implementing a new approach to environmental management typically involves a series of specific changes that can easily extend the period of change beyond a decade. And again, over time, change in a learning organization never ends.

We argue that proactive commercial firms often speak of effective environmental management as being more an attitude and approach than a formal program. In these firms, effective environmental management becomes a commitment embedded in the organization to seek high-quality performance and then sustain it through continuing learning and improvement. Such a commitment provides a context for a series of specific changes:

- These firms choose specific changes that they can build on for future learning. If they own multiple plants and pursue multiple activities at each plant, they may target environmental management of one activity in each plant. An activity at one plant serves as a "seed" for extending change to analogous activities at other plants; it also acts as a seed to extend changes to other activities at the same plant.

- To identify such seed activities at plants, these firms seek lower-risk, higher-payoff changes first. This approach seeks early successes to give change momentum. It limits the cost of incremental failures, making it easier to "fail forward."

- These firms develop a well-defined plan for each change at the location where it will occur. The plan may extend over several years and may change during that period, but it changes against a set of planning milestones that provide a basis for accountability.

We note that no specific change locks the organization into a future it cannot alter. These firms recognize the need to continue looking beyond each specific change to a broader commitment to flexibility and learning.

This pattern of change has three important implications for DoD. First, almost all commercial firms are small relative to DoD. Efforts to induce change throughout DoD will in all likelihood take even longer than they do in any large commercial firm. Second, the senior leadership in OSD and the military departments and defense agencies is typically less stable than in large commercial firms. It is very unlikely that any leadership team in DoD could see a significant organizationwide change through from conception to full implementation during its tenure. Hence, to achieve significant organizationwide change, DoD must give more attention to institutionalizing the change *process* than commercial firms do. The leaders should eschew the temptation to achieve some small substantive policy change that they will be remembered for in favor of nurturing a new organizational process that will ultimately generate many substantive policy changes over time.

Third, DoD has experience with such change management. In any major weapon system acquisition program office (SPO), modifications induced by continuing learning persist through the life of the

---

Example 33

Ford: A Staged Approach for Global Registration to ISO 14001

Building on its experience with ISO 9000, Ford used an incremental approach to implementing a new corporatewide environmental policy that carefully and systematically managed risk and built on success. Its initial movement toward registering plants to ISO 14001 began at individual plants in Europe. Fortified by the demonstrated value of these isolated actions, Ford brought the manager responsible to its worldwide headquarters to pursue a much broader program. In North America, Ford first targeted five plants with two important attributes:

1. Each conducted a core activity relevant to Ford's worldwide automobile operations—engine manufacturing, transmission manufacturing, electronics manufacturing, aluminum manufacturing, and vehicle assembly.

2. Each had already demonstrated an ability to introduce innovative processes on a large scale.

Ford carefully monitored implementation at these plants and developed lessons learned relevant to similar plants elsewhere. Through this carefully staged process, Ford was ultimately able to certify about 140 plants, employing 200,000 employees worldwide, in about two years.

system.[1] At any time, under normal circumstances, the SPO may be managing tens or hundreds of modifications. "Basket" SPOs that manage a family of related systems, such as engines or transport aircraft, remain in place indefinitely, managing the development and modification of one system after another. The champion for change actions associated with environmental management might use a similar structure to manage the many elements of such changes. Such a champion would have to understand, of course, that organizational acceptance of a specific change is at least as important to success as technical response to a combat contingency is in a traditional weapon SPO. Proactive environmental management is primarily about organizational, not technological, change. The centralized champion must mobilize and motivate technical specialists throughout the organization to make the organization as a whole effectively proactive.

---

[1]Compare the concept of managing implementation as an innovation process in Leonard-Barton (1996), p. 92.

Chapter Six

RECOMMENDATION:
USE FORMAL QUALITY FRAMEWORKS TO
IMPLEMENT AN INTEGRATION POLICY

The discussion above leads to the conclusion that DoD can benefit from using total quality management (TQM) to plan and implement the integration of environmental management with core its concerns. At its heart, TQM within a DoD context can be thought of as a three-part technique (Levine and Luck, 1994; cf. Womack and Jones, 1996):

- Identify DoD's key stakeholders and what each wants.

- Identify the processes that ultimately serve each stakeholder and map their interrelationships (for example, core product design and production processes; infrastructure support processes; remediation processes; and the associated material management, recycling, treatment, disposal, training, research and development, and compliance processes).

- Work continuously to remove "waste" from these processes to give DoD's stakeholders more of what they want (anything that does not add value to what a stakeholder wants is waste; emissions and the activities they require are typically quintessential forms of waste under TQM).

Formal, quality-based methods have been developed to pursue these goals by doing many of the things that proactive commercial firms are doing. That is hardly surprising. U.S. firms finally learned the value of applying TQM in the 1980s. As they met success with the improvement of their core processes, pioneers began to see the connection between reducing waste and reducing emissions. Early applications of TQM to emission reduction helped build the case for the new proactive corporate approach to environmental management discussed above. Since then, many other firms have applied TQM more broadly to pursue a program of environmental management very much like that mapped above.[1] DoD might profitably consider a similar approach.

AVAILABLE FORMAL QUALITY FRAMEWORKS

Initial efforts to implement TQM in U.S. firms led to a lot of sloganeering and few tangible results. Firms had great difficulty translating the broad, imprecise guidelines used to define TQM into specific management practices that produced the results TQM promises. Early DoD experiments with TQM at defense-contractor facilities produced similar results. Cynicism was a common response.

That changed as firms began to try again with ISO 9000. ISO 9000 is a family of auditing tools that ISO developed to define exactly what a firm has to do to implement real TQM.[2] ISO certifies third-party auditors, who in turn apply standardized accounting methods to determine whether a firm has in fact changed its internal processes in a way that implements TQM. As these third-party auditors looked over their shoulders, firms began to achieve the desired outcomes. By the early 1990s, firms reported such significant successes with ISO 9000 that it became a standard requirement for qualifying suppliers in many industries. The U.S. automobile industry, long known for its detailed quality standards for suppliers, actually adjusted its old qualification standards to use ISO 9000 as a baseline and issued the QS9000 supplier-qualification standards that build on ISO 9000 (Perry Johnson, Inc., 1995, pp. 61–65). The aerospace industry is following suit with AS-9000.

Meanwhile, other firms found that they could improve on ISO 9000 in their internal activities. Although they had third-party auditors certify their compliance with ISO 9000, they found they could apply

---

[1]For examples, see Willig (1994).

[2]At its heart are three "quality systems" or "contractual models" approved in 1987: 9001 is the most comprehensive and covers design and development, production, installation, and servicing of products; 9002 covers production and installation of products; and 9003 covers final inspection and test of products. Other guidelines explain the auditing approach itself and define how audits will occur. Many good references are available; see, for example, Johnson (1993).

TQM concepts even more extensively with even more-dramatic effects on productivity. As firms learned to do this, some came to doubt the usefulness of ISO 9000. Why spend the considerable sum required to achieve third-party certification if you could do even better without ISO 9000? These firms turned their sights on the Malcolm Baldrige Award, established by Congress in 1987, to certify an even higher level of achievement.[3] ISO 9000 came to offer certification to external customers that a firm had implemented the basic elements of TQM, while the Baldrige Award offered evidence that a firm had gone well beyond the basics to become one of the best-quality firms in the United States.[4]

As firms discovered the usefulness of TQM concepts for improving environmental management, they turned to the formal frameworks offered by the ISO 9000 program and the Baldrige Award criteria for aid in refining their environmental management programs. In 1990, about 20 major firms formed GEMI, with the specific intention of formalizing something they called total quality environmental management (TQEM). GEMI participants have all documented dramatic benefits associated with their own variations on TQEM. At about the same time, the Council of Great Lakes Industries began to develop its own quality-based implementation techniques. Building on the Baldrige Award criteria, the council developed its own framework for TQEM and supported it with a primer and case studies in 1993 (Wever and Vorhauer, 1993). The resulting TQEM matrix provides the basis for a detailed assessment of a firm's application of quality techniques to its environmental management program.[5]

Building on efforts to apply TQM concepts to environmental management issues in Europe, ISO began developing a new family of

---

[3]The details of the Baldrige approach change each year. For the most up-to-date information available, see the Baldrige links at http://www.quality.nist.gov.

[4]A recent analysis showed that the 16 publicly owned firms that have won the Baldrige Award have outperformed the Standard and Poor's 500-stock index by three to one in terms of return on investment. The 48 publicly owned firms that made it to the final round in the Baldrige Award outperformed the Standard and Poor's 500-stock index by two to one (Port, 1997).

[5]For a detailed discussion of this approach, how to apply it, and how it compares with the other quality frameworks discussed here, see Wever (1996).

audit-based guidelines called ISO 14000.[6] The members of ISO finally reached agreement on the first specific guideline from this family, ISO 14001, in 1996. Other elements of ISO 14000 are expected to be approved over the next few years but will act more as guidelines than as requirements. Like ISO 9000, ISO 14000 calls for a detailed audit of the management processes that an organization uses, in this case, to implement a formal environmental management system. Critics claim ISO 14001 is not as comprehensive as its ISO 9000 predecessors or as demanding as the major voluntary European environmental auditing systems based on ISO 9000. ISO 14001 does not require third-party auditing and does not commit a user to a proactive pollution prevention program. Nonetheless, U.S. and foreign firms are giving ISO 14001 close attention as a useful framework for implementing a basic TQM approach to environmental management

Example 34

Ford and IBM: Choosing Third-Party Registration to ISO 14001

Unlike many other large, U.S. industrial firms, Ford and IBM both decided to use ISO 14001, not only as a template against which to benchmark their preexisting environmental management systems but also as a certificate to verify to potential customers their level of environmental responsibility. Both agreed to do this for similar reasons:

1. Many of their customers, particularly in Europe and East Asia, appeared likely to favor such certification.

2. Given the sophistication of their preexisting environmental management systems, moving to full registration against the standard was unlikely to be terribly difficult.

That said, Ford estimated that it spent $220,000 for training and 5,600 hours of employee time for meetings, training, and audits to register one engine manufacturing plant. At the same time, despite the sophistication of the baseline environmental management system at that site, the new system based on ISO 14001 supported large, immediate improvements in water use, solid waste generation, and use of returnable packaging. Early gap analysis identified several places where ISO 14001 would improve the effectiveness and efficiency of IBM's preexisting environmental management system and further integrate environmental considerations around the company. These gains may not have occurred without third-party registration.

---

[6]Jackson (1995) discusses the European systems underlying the ISO 14000 series.

or certifying that a firm has done so. Regulators throughout the United States and elsewhere are also studying how to use ISO 14000 as the basis for a form of regulation that would give regulated organizations more control over how they reduce their environmental emissions and waste. As more organizations have certified themselves to ISO 14000, global attention has increasingly shifted to ISO 14000 from the more-aggressive European alternatives.[7]

All these frameworks respond to a desire to implement quality-based methods systematically. Some (ISO 9000 and Baldrige) address a broad range of management concerns; others (TQEM and ISO 14000) focus on environmental management per se. Some (ISO 9000 and 14000) require entry-level compliance with TQM practices; others (Baldrige and TQEM) seek to drive world-class performance. The broad acceptance these efforts have achieved among proactive commercial firms speaks to the need for assistance in implementing broad management principles whose success depends heavily on their proper implementation.

Tables 1 through 3 summarize in very broad terms how these formal quality frameworks address the issues raised in the sections above.[8] Table 1 addresses the key policy challenge of integrating environmental missions and functions with core missions and functions; Table 2, the challenge of effecting change when no silver bullets are available to address a wide range of different situations; and Table 3, the challenge of sustaining support for radical organizational change that necessarily takes a long time to complete. The tables reveal that these quality frameworks do not require any user to do all the things discussed above. But the frameworks help create a well-defined, structured management context that makes it far more likely that a firm will succeed in its efforts to do these things.

---

[7]For useful discussions of the pros and cons of using ISO 14000 to create a new approach to regulation, see Begley (1996) and Butner (1996).

[8]The frameworks included in this discussion are ISO 9001, ISO 14001, the Malcolm Baldrige Award criteria, and the Council of Great Lakes Industries' TQEM Implementation Guide and Assessment Matrix (in Wever, 1996). Specific references to TQEM in the table refer to the Baldrige Award criteria and the TQEM assessment framework based on it.

Table 1

Use Formal Quality Frameworks to Support the Key Policy Challenge: Integrate Environmental Missions and Functions with Core Missions and Functions

Appropriate Approaches	How Formal Quality Frameworks Support Improved Approaches
Task: Identify stakeholders and related goals	
Require clear statement of goals and related objectives; constructively involve key stakeholders	Frameworks reward statement of goals that link environment to core strategic values; TQEM directly involves stakeholders
Task: Maintain senior leadership support	
Define environmental outcomes in terms leadership can understand; institutionalize processes that ensure leadership is always well informed on key environmental matters	ISO instruments verify that an effective, auditable review cycle exists; TQEM encourages use of effective metrics and strategic engagement of the leadership
Task: Give environmental champions day-to-day responsibility	
Choose champions for personal qualities and core experience and empower them; clearly define their roles and responsibilities	Frameworks do not require champions, but effective use of champions promotes an emphasis on effective roles and responsibilities, alignment to process, and cross-organizational coordination
Task: Build coalitions with other internal interests	
Link environmental management to broader quality efforts; use these to support cross-department understanding of the value of improved environmental performance	Frameworks at their hearts are quality-based systems and support cross-department efforts to pursue process improvement
Task: Integrate relevant elements of value chain	
Align make-or-buy decisions with general organizational goals, specific risks, and ability to manage risks; choose compatible partners; and integrate processes and data with them	Frameworks do not support this directly but favor (1) sourcing and contracting processes aligned with strategic goals and key environmental aspects and the (2) continuous improvement that this approach encourages

Table 1—Continued

Appropriate Approaches	How Formal Quality Frameworks Support Improved Approaches
Task: State environmental goals in simple, specific terms	
Choose terms that are easy for the relevant players who must change or monitor change to understand and measure	Frameworks encourage this when they link goals to objectives and metrics; compatible with TQEM emphasis on empowering human resources
Task: Use cross-functional teams for specific decisions, projects, etc.	
Align teams to processes that cut across organizational units; train, empower team members to make decisions for their departments	Quality frameworks require clear linkages between processes and related functions; teams aligned with processes support this approach
Task: Develop tools to identify firmwide effects of environmental activities	
Develop metrics that link environmental activities to core values; in particular, use activity-based costing to remove environmental costs from indirect cost pools	Quality frameworks require documentation of templates and databases; TQEM seeks feedback on environmental effects throughout the firm
Task: Balance centralization and decentralization	
Align the degree of centralization of environmental management with broader organizational goals on centralization	Frameworks do not directly care about centralization but reward efforts to align environmental management with core business processes and decisions

Table 2

Use Formal Quality Frameworks to Support Implementation Challenge 1: There Are No Silver Bullets When Every Situation Is Different

Appropriate Approaches	How Formal Quality Frameworks Support Improved Approaches
Task: Motivate creative and persistent change agents	
Maintain focus at all levels on outcomes; align incentives of those who must change with outcome measures	Frameworks support effective links between business goals, processes, and incentives
Task: Assign responsibilities clearly throughout the firm	
Define and align authority and responsibility of each person who must change; identify disconnects and correct them quickly as improvement proceeds	Frameworks require clear mapping of roles and responsibility; in particular, frameworks reward process cycles that keep leadership informed and adjust policies as needed over time
Task: Design metrics to motivate the right behavior	
Distinguish motivational and diagnostic metrics; ensure that motivational metrics reflect what each player can affect	Frameworks link metrics to goals and objectives and document databases that feed metrics
Task: Use incentives to motivate the right behavior	
Align incentives so that those who must change benefit if they change appropriately and suffer if they do not	TQEM seeks to link a system of rewards and consequences to all aspects of environmental management
Task: Manage failures to limit disincentives for risk-taking	
Monitor change to catch errors quickly; emphasize the value of exposing errors to learn organizational lessons from them; reward error-reporting if it supports "failing forward"	Frameworks do not support this directly, but it is compatible with a well-defined process that learns over time and reacts quickly and constructively to failures; frameworks reward these attributes
Task: Empower employees with formal training	
Train employees regularly, continually; train on group process, problem solving, innovation, as well as process substance; monitor the value added from training	Frameworks require documentation of training; TQEM explicitly seeks effective training program; frameworks reward links between training and core goals

Table 2—Continued

Appropriate Approaches	How Formal Quality Frameworks Support Improved Approaches
Task: Develop a supportive organizational context for tools	
Use simple tools that yield effective operational improvements to start, then use "spiral development" for new tools, progressively testing and improving them in an operational setting	Frameworks do not support this directly; but it is compatible with quality-based improvement cycles focused on process improvements that effect real outcomes; and frameworks support such cycles
Task: Communicate continuously in all directions	
Communicate up to engage leaders; communicate down to motivate change; communicate sideways to diffuse success stories and lessons learned	Frameworks require documentation of communication plan and activities; effective communication supports broader improvement goals of frameworks
Task: Manage relationships with stakeholders	
Engage them to maintain focus and avoid surprises from interested parties; prevent any one player from capturing control; use core values to balance players	TQEM seeks deep interaction with stakeholders on environmental management
Task: Benchmark to promote continuous improvement	
Continually monitor developments outside the organization; use them to set goals; define and maintain metrics that support easy, reliable, continual comparisons	Encouraged by all frameworks; required for Baldrige, high levels under TQEM

Table 3

**Use Formal Quality Frameworks to Support Implementation Challenge 2:
Radical Organizational Change Takes a Long Time**

Appropriate Approaches	How Formal Quality Frameworks Support Improved Approaches
Task: Institutionalize framework for long-term continuous improvement	
Build SPO-like offices to use standing structures to manage a series of linked, accumulating changes; focus these offices on managing organizational, not technical, change and risk	Frameworks require a continuous improvement cycle that supports this task; ISO audit regimes seek clear documentation of such cycles and the data they manage
Task: Design and manage specific change actions	
Create flexible action, development, or "war" plans with clear goals, metrics, milestones, roles, and responsibilities; align these with investment, incentive, training, tool, and communication plans	Frameworks do not support this directly, but it is hard to execute the improvement cycles, high-level review, and process alignment that frameworks encourage without such plans
Task: Start with low-risk, high-payoff changes and build on success	
Initiate change far from core activities to limit risk to core and change processes; use incremental successes to validate and sustain support for continuing change	Frameworks do not support this directly, but commercial experience indicates that such an approach supports the continuous improvement that frameworks seek

FORMAL QUALITY FRAMEWORKS FOR DOD

Informal discussions about using ISO 9000 to improve productivity have occurred in many different parts of DoD. Although ISO 9000 offers an attractive set of guidelines that could be applied as easily to a government activity as to a commercial firm, DoD has resisted allowing a third-party auditor to review its implementation of these guidelines. Commercial experience strongly suggests, however, that, until an organization has in fact mastered the TQM basics embodied in ISO 9000, it is hard to implement TQM without outside oversight.

DoD's interest in implementing environmental management policies like those that leading commercial firms advocate offers an opportunity to reopen this question from a different perspective. Although DoD's reluctance to use ISO 9000 is a serious problem, it is worth reviewing the broad benefits that DoD adoption of ISO 9000 might offer:

- ISO 9000 is a widely accepted commercial standard. Using such an approach is compatible with formal support for greater reliance on commercial standards in DoD and renewed interest in exploiting best commercial practices to reengineer the support infrastructure.[9]

- ISO 9000 has been successfully adopted by very large, multinational, multidivisional firms that share attributes with DoD relevant to its diversity and global presence.

- ISO 9000 can be applied incrementally to individual functions at individual DoD locations. This allows pilot testing that can then act as a seed for broader application if it works as expected. ISO 9000 is fully scalable to organizations of very large size and, in practice, has been more useful in larger firms facing more-daunting implementation problems.

- ISO 9000 offers an explicit way in which the Deputy Under Secretary of Defense (Environmental Security) can build a coalition with a broader community in DoD to promote process improvement. The processes in question touch almost every

---

[9]See, for example, Commission on Roles and Missions of the Armed Forces (1995) and U.S. DoD (1996).

part of DoD, including acquisition, logistics, medical services, base operating support, office and housing services, and cleanup. ISO 9000 offers a formal way to link implementation of the under secretary's policy goals to process improvement in all these areas.

- Current DoD policy envisions expanded reliance on private sources of support services. If this occurs, ISO 9000 will offer a natural platform for building effective relationships with high-quality private sources. This applies to sources of environmental and other services and supplies.

All these statements could also be made about using the Baldrige Award criteria, but ISO 9000 is normally viewed as a natural stepping stone toward world-class performance. ISO 9000 also offers a natural stepping stone toward the use of ISO 14000, which may offer new opportunities to DoD in its relationships with regulators and private sources of services and supplies. Although one firm suggested that DoD could seek ISO 9000 and 14000 certification for its activities simultaneously, most proactive commercial firms envision moving from a well-established ISO 9000 platform in place today to ISO 14000 at some point in the future when its usefulness becomes more apparent.

Example 35

IBM: Single Worldwide Registration to ISO 14001

IBM's direct, active participation in the development of ISO 14001 probably made it easier to take an aggressive approach to ISO 14001. Following piece-meal, plant-initiated registrations of five plants in the United Kingdom, Japan, and Singapore and the registrations of several other sites to the European Eco-Management and Audit Scheme (EMAS), IBM turned to the provision in the brand-new formal version of ISO 14001 that allowed an organization to acquire a single worldwide registration for all of its sites. This approach allowed an organization to start the registration process by auditing and registering a representative sample of its sites under a single environmental management system. The organization could then add additional sites to the registration as they completed their audits and registrations. Of 28 headquarters, manufacturing, and R&D sites included in the plan, IBM registered 11 within one year, 26 within two years, and all within three years. IBM was the first firm to use this approach to worldwide registration on this scale.

Which of these DoD might select to test for broader application is less important than the fact that all offer existing and readily available frameworks for helping DoD take the next step in its efforts to improve defense environmental management. Its current policies are broadly compatible with the best practices we observe in the commercial sector. To implement these policies, DoD should give careful thought to following the approaches these firms have taken to implementation. Proactive firms have relied heavily on formal quality frameworks. These frameworks helped the firms verify that they were implementing their intended policies. The frameworks also helped verify that the firms were indeed staying on the course the policies had set and would continue to do so for the long haul. Large organizations must have the long-term staying power required to change and to learn the best ways of integrating environmental and core concerns.

BIBLIOGRAPHY

Bardach, Eugene, *The Implementation Game*, Cambridge, Mass.: Massachusetts Institute of Technology Press, 1979.

Begley, Ronald, "ISO 14000: A Step Toward Industry Self-Regulation," *Environmental Science and Technology*, Vol. 30, No. 7, 1996, pp. 298–302.

Berube, Michael, et al., "From Pollution Control to Zero Discharge: How the Robbins Company Overcame the Obstacles," *Pollution Prevention Review*, Spring 1992, pp. 189–207.

Blumenfeld, Karen, and Anthony Montrone, "Environmental Strategy—Stepping Up to Business Demands," *Prism*, 4th Quarter 1995, pp. 79–90.

Butner, Scott, "ISO 14000—Policy and Regulatory Implications for State Agencies," *National Pollution Prevention Roundtable, Spring National Meeting*, Washington, D.C., April 1996, pp. 1–8.

Camm, Frank, *Environmental Management in Proactive Commercial Firms: Lessons for Central Logistics Activities in the Department of Defense*, Santa Monica, Calif.: RAND, MR-1308-OSD, 2001.

Clarke, Richard A., et al., "The Challenge of Going Green," *Harvard Business Review*, July–August 1994, pp. 37–50.

Commission on Roles and Missions of the Armed Forces, *Directions for Defense*, Washington, D.C.: U.S. Government Printing Office, 1995.

Defense Science Board, *Report of the Defense Science Board Task Force on Environmental Security,* Washington, D.C., Office of the Under Secretary of Defense for Acquisition and Technology, 1995.

Drezner, Jeffrey, and Frank Camm, *Using Process Design to Improve DoD's Environmental Security Program: Remediation Program Management,* Santa Monica, Calif.: RAND, MR-1024-OSD, 1999.

Ehrfeld, John R., and Jennifer Howard, "Setting Environmental Goals: A Review of Practices from the 60's to the Present," unpublished manuscript, Cambridge, Mass.: Massachusetts Institute of Technology Program on Technology, Business, and Environment, 1995.

Global Environmental Management Initiative, *Benchmarking, the Primer: Benchmarking for Continuous Environmental Improvement,* Washington, D.C., 1994.

"The Green Machine: Environmental Regulations and Responsibilities Becoming More Important," *Quality Progress,* March 1995, pp. 17–18.

Greeno, J. Ladd, et al., "Rethinking the Environment for Business Advantage, *Prism,* 1st Quarter 1996, pp. 5–15.

Hoffman, Andrew, "Teaching Old Dogs New Tricks: Creating Incentives for Industry to Adopt Pollution Prevention," *Pollution Prevention Review,* Winter 1992–93, pp. 1–11.

Jackson, Suzan L., "Certification of Environmental Management Systems—for ISO 9000 and Competitive Advantage," in Willig (ed.), 1995, pp. 61–69.

Johnson, Perry L., *ISO 9000: Meeting the New International Standards,* New York: McGraw-Hill, Inc., 1993.

Kaplan, Robert S., ed., *Measures for Manufacturing Excellence,* Boston: Harvard Business School Press, 1990.

Kaplan, Robert S., and David P. Norton, *The Balanced Scorecard: Translating Strategy into Action,* Boston: Harvard Business School Press, 1996.

Kaplan, Robert S., and David P. Norton, *The Strategy-Focused Organization: How Balanced Scorecard Companies Thrive in the*

New Business Environment, Boston: Harvard Business School Press, 2000.

Kirchenstein, John J., and Rodger A. Jump, "The European Eco-Label and Audit Scheme: New Environmental Standards for Competing Abroad," in Willig (ed.), 1995, pp. 70–78.

Kotter, John P., *Leading Change*, Boston: Harvard Business School Press, 1996.

Lachman, Beth E., Frank Camm, and Susan A. Resetar, *Integrated Facility Approaches to Environmental Management: Industry Lessons Learned for Department of Defense Facilities*, Santa Monica, Calif.: RAND, MR-1343-OSD, 2001.

Leonard-Barton, Dorothy, *Wellsprings of Knowledge*, Boston: Harvard Business School Press, 1996.

Levine, Arnold, and Jeffrey Luck, *The New Management Paradigm: A Review of Principles and Practices*, Santa Monica, Calif.: RAND, MR-458-AF, 1994.

Nagel, George, "Business Environmental Cost Accounting Survey," in Global Environmental Management Initiative, *Environmental Management in a Global Economy*, Washington, D.C., 1994.

Ochsner, Michele, Caron Chess, and Michael Greenberg, "Case Study: DuPont's Edge Moore Facility," *Pollution Prevention Review*, Winter 1995–96, p. 71.

Perry Johnson, Inc., "QS-9000—Quality," *Automotive Engineering*, June 1995, pp. 61–65.

Piasecki, Bruce, *Corporate Environmental Strategy*, New York: John Wiley and Sons, 1995.

Port, Otis, "The Baldrige's Other Reward," *Business Week*, March 10, 1997, p. 75.

Porter, Michael E., and Claas van den Linde, "Green and Competitive: Ending the Stalemate," *Harvard Business Review*, September–October 1995, pp. 120–133.

Resetar, Susan A., Frank Camm, and Jeffrey A. Drezner, *Environmental Management in Design: Lessons from Volvo and Hewlett-Packard for the Department of Defense*, Santa Monica, Calif.: RAND, MR-1009-OSD, 1998.

Rubenson, David, et al., *Marching to Different Drummers: Evolution of the Army's Environmental Program*, Santa Monica, Calif.: RAND, MR-453-A, 1994.

Starik, Mark, Alfred A. Marcus, and Anne Y. Ilinitch (eds.), "Special Research Forum on the Management of Organizations in the Natural Environment," *Academy of Management Journal*, Vol. 43, No. 43, August 2000, pp. 535–737.

Superfund Amendments and Reauthorization Act (1986), Sec. 313.

U.S. Bureau of the Census, *Statistical Abstract of the United States, 1996*, 116th ed., Washington, D.C., 1996.

U.S. Department of Defense, Office of the USD for Acquisition and Technology, *Achieving an Innovative Support Structure for Twenty-First Century Military Superiority: Higher Performance at Lower Costs*, Washington, D.C., 1996.

Walley, Noah, and Bradley Whitehead, "It's Not Easy Being Green," *Harvard Business Review*, May–June 1994, pp. 46–52.

Wever, Grace H., *Strategic Environment Management: Using TQEM and ISO 14000 for Competitive Advantage*, New York: John Wiley and Sons, 1996.

Wever, Grace H., and George F. Vorhauer, "Kodak's Framework and Assessment Tool for Implementing TQEM," *Total Quality Environmental Management*, Autumn 1993, pp. 19–30.

Williams, Walter, *The Implementation Perspective*, Berkeley: University of California Press, 1980.

Willig, John T., *Environmental TQM*, 2nd ed., New York: McGraw-Hill, 1994.

Willig, John T., *Auditing for Environmental Quality Leadership*, New York: John Wiley and Sons, 1995.

Womack, James P., and Daniel T. Jones, *Lean Thinking*, New York: Simon and Schuster, 1996.

Zellman, Gail L., "Implementing Policy Change in Large Organizations," in National Defense Research Institute, *Sexual Orientation and U.S. Military Personnel Policy: Options and Assessment*, Santa Monica, Calif.: RAND, MR-323-OSD, 1993.